Scrapbooking Digitally

by being your self you put some thing wonder ful in the world that was not there before

Dagmar Wagner

Scrapbooking Digitally

The Ultimate Guide to Saving Your Memories Digitally

Kerry Arquette, Darlene D'Agostino, Susha Roberts, & Andrea Zocchi

cantata books

The Taunton Press

Executive Editor
Kerry Arquette

Editor
Darlene D'Agostino

Technical Editor
Susha Roberts

Art Director/Designer
Andrea Zocchi

Cover Design
Peter Horjus

Production Designer
Susha Roberts

Copy Editor
Dena Twinem

The Taunton Press, Inc., 63 South Main Street,
PO Box 5506, Newtown, CT 06470-5506
e-mail: tp@taunton.com

Library of Congress Cataloging-in-Publication Data
Scrapbooking digitally : the ultimate guide to saving your memories digitally / executive editor, Kerry Arquette.
     p. cm.
  Includes bibliographical references and index.
  ISBN 978-1-56158-972-2 (alk. paper)
 1. Photographs--Conservation and restoration--Data processing. 2. Photography--Digital techniques. 3. Photo-
graph albums--Data processing. 4. Scrapbooks--Data processing. 5. Digital preservation. I. Arquette, Kerry.

TR465.S39375 2007
771'.460285--dc22

                    2007018134

Printed in Singapore

Created and produced
by Cantata Books Inc.
P.O. Box 307
Englewood, CO 80151
www.cantatabooks.com

Dedication

When embarking on this project, we felt more like "digital ditzes" than "digital divas." To educate ourselves we buddied up with Photoshop Elements manuals, plowed through hours of tutorials, and humbly sought advice from software experts and our artists. We tested the limits of Andrea's patience by inundating him with questions like: "Why is my computer doing THIS when I want it to do THAT?" only to bark at him moments later that we really didn't MEAN or CARE about the "why." We just wanted the darn thing to cooperate.

We apologize publicly to Andrea, and thank him and Susha, our technical editor, for keeping us on track. That said, this book is dedicated to anyone who ever thought that they couldn't do something, to those who have upon occasion cowered in the face of a challenge, to anybody who has felt that something was just too much work to be worth learning. Remember, the biggest obstacle to overcome in learning to digitally scrapbook is not the technology; it is ourselves.

This book also goes out to anyone who's ever felt the need to launch a computer manual from a third floor window. Those manuals are notoriously difficult to understand, filled with information that clutters and complicates rather than clarifies. We hope that every bit of the information you find in this book will be hands-on helpful. We'd also like to dedicate this book to the amazing artists whose work appears in these pages. Without their creative and pioneering vision, this project would not have been possible. Oh, and to our families and friends: Thanks for putting up with the late suppers, the worked weekends, the colorful language, the kicking and screaming, and the glazed-over faces.

Sheila Doherty

Table of Contents

Going Digital
Now I'm footloose & fancy free

I am flipping for digital scrapbooking! It keeps my budget intact & is much easier than I thought it would be to create bright, fun layouts. I can make my own digital elements without having to rush to the store for more supplies. And kits I buy online have unlimited possibilities. I'm able to change the colors with ease to meet my needs. Digital Scrapbooking Rocks!

Shannon Taylor

Go Digital, Darlin'!

Digi darlin's are the kind of crafters who look forward, anticipating the next challenge as an adventure. While they may harbor deep affection for their traditional scrapbook pages and the warm experiences they associate with creating them, it is the jazzy digital world that floats their boat these days.

Ask any digi scrapper why she's chosen to preserve her memories the modern way and she's likely to e-mail you a variety of cutting-edge scrapbook pages. These layouts vibrate with the unique personality of a scrapbooker unbridled by the limitations of traditional scrapbook supplies, a scrapbooker who can alter photos, colors, shapes, patterns, and the placement of elements to her heart's content. And, if her scrapbook page defiantly refuses to gel, she can hit the Delete button to banish it to The Great Beyond.

Traditional scrapbookers thinking about stepping into the digi world can do it in baby steps by learning new ways to use their digital camera or include computer-written journaling on their pages. Modern technology makes everything so easy—everyone can find a manageable learning curve. Remember, a little digital daring today will make you tomorrow's digital diva.

The Perks of Digital
Cutting back on expenses, crafting space, and time

Although learning to digitally scrapbook may force you outside of your comfort zone as you learn new skills, you'll find the long-term benefits far outweigh any immediate qualms. So take a deep breath and just take that first step forward. Before you know it, you'll be looking back over your shoulder and wondering why you ever believed the path would be difficult to navigate.

Save Cash
When a traditional scrapbooker uses a brad, it is gone. She must buy more when her next page calls for a brad. Digital supplies, on the other hand, can be used on an endless number of subsequent layouts. The color and size of digital supplies can be easily altered, so you have countless design options. Now that's more bang for your buck.

In this page the artist used brads and embellishments from a number of different digital kits. All these elements may be used again and again and altered as desired.

Leah Blanco Williams, Photo: Thomas Williams

The fine Art of **joke-telling**

Lucas: Knock-knock.

Tyler: Knock-knock!

Lucas: No, you say "Who's there?"

Tyler: Who's there!

Lucas: Coo-coo!

Tyler: HA! HA! *(loud, fake laugh)*

Lucas: No, Ty! Don't laugh yet. You say, "Coo-coo, *who?*"

Tyler: Who?

Lucas: No, your 'posed to say, "Coo-coo, WHO!"

Traditional or digital? Only the artist knows for sure! One of these pages was created with lifelike digital supplies, while the other was made with traditional scrapbook papers, brads, and a sticker.

The fine Art of **joke-telling**

Lucas: Knock-knock.

Tyler: Knock-knock!

Lucas: No, you say "Who's there?"

Tyler: Who's there!

Lucas: Coo-coo!

Tyler: HA! HA! *(loud, fake laugh)*

Lucas: No, Ty! Don't laugh yet. You say, "Coo-coo, *who?*"

Tyler: *Who?*

Lucas: No, you 'posed to say, "Coo-coo, WHO!"

Tyler: Coo-coo who?

Lucas: Coo-coo-be-ba-boo!

Much laughter & squealing in delight from both boys.

Sheila Doherty

Save Space

Your digital scrapbooking station fits well into any nook within your home. You may find yourself scrapbooking in your home office, or repurposing a seldom-used corner or closet. Even a small space can be turned into a digital crop room big enough to hold a computer, printer, and scanner. With some vertical shelving, you can add storage space for a tidy collection of traditional papers and other supplies you may wish to use on your printed computer-generated layouts.

Because digital scrapbooking provides maximum effect with only minimal supplies, messy scrapbooking spaces are history.

10 Reasons HE ♥ His Digital Scrapbooker

- The dining room table (freed from its layers of scrapbook papers) can once again be used for guys' poker night.
- No more humiliating discoveries that he's got stickers clinging to the soles of his work shoes.
- The inviting image gracing the family computer screen makes doing bills a happy occasion (almost).
- Never again will dinner be delayed by a last-minute stop at the scrapbooking store so you could "just take a peek."
- No more arguments over the time saving merits (or not) of spending $80 on identically patterned papers in different colors.

- Boring family portraits are replaced by artful collages of family photos.
- You can now downsize houses and mortgages since a full-sized crop room is no longer necessary.
- That digitally altered image you created using his boss's head and a monkey makes him grin.
- No more shutting down the airport because SOMEBODY forgot to remove her craft knife from her carry-on.
- You look so darn cute rockin' out with headphones and a laptop at the kitchen table or on the family room couch.

Save Time

Shopping for traditional scrapbooking supplies requires a trip to the store and time cruising the aisles, or days waiting for supplies you've ordered online to be received through the mail. As a digital scrapbooker, you can shop for supplies online, downloading them for immediate use. And while traditional scrapbookers spend time pulling out their materials and then cleaning and restoring them after each scrapbooking session, you need only drag and drop supplies into organized folders and switch on and off your computer. Sharing your work with family and friends is quick and easy as well. You'll no longer find yourself hunting down packing materials and stamps when you can post your photos to an online gallery and your projects to scrapbooking Web sites. Those interested can visit the sites to enjoy your latest photos and scrapbook pages.

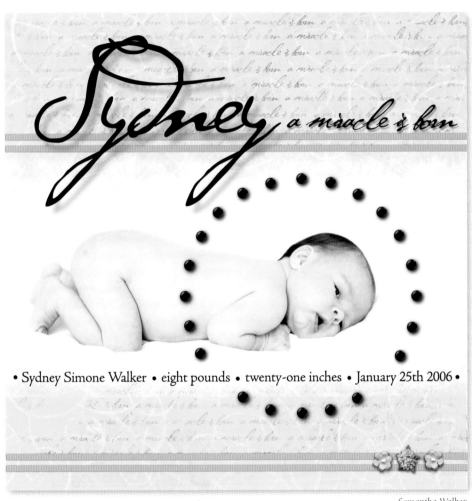

Samantha Walker

This digital layout does double duty. For Mom, it's a beautiful layout for Baby's album. For family, it's a beautiful birth announcement. Mom, ever so savvy, also created a matching thank-you card simultaneously to save additional time and money.

Samantha Walker

I wonder when it happened? When exactly did my wish lists change from novels and paintbrushes to EHD's and RAM? When did I start longing for new camera filters and tripods while my friends were longing for new shoes? When did I begin to love this stuff so much?

And I really do love it all; my sleek Wacom tablet, my treasured iMac and of course my beloved camera. I am happiest when surrounded by my digital treasures, my tools of the trade, the stuff I couldn't scrap without.

Mary-Ann Buchanan

The Digital Craft Room

When designing your first digital layout, the difference between sinking and swimming rests upon preparation. Ease into the activity by learning everything you can about the technical aspects of the craft. Once a solid understanding is in place, rookie mistakes can be avoided.

This chapter introduces you to the world of digital. Along with some basic techniques, you'll find "good to know" information about your computer and its components, handy technical vocabulary, and the ins/outs/ups/downs/points/clicks of common menus and tools. Learn how to set up an efficient digital crop space, and get the lowdown on suggested digital products. When you've completed this chapter, you'll be well prepared to dive into digital memory keeping with confidence.

Spaces and Places

Setting up your computer, peripherals, and scrapbooking supplies

Even if you have a laptop and consider yourself a strictly on-the-go digital scrapbooker, you'll want a home base to park your computer when it's not traveling with you. Many scrapbookers use their home offices as creative zones. Others turn seldom-used corners or closets into scrapping areas. Optimally, your digital design area will have the horizontal and vertical space you need for hardware, supporting supplies, and storage. It must have access to electrical outlets for a power strip with a surge protector. Your digital crop area will be your comfortable and very personal sanctuary from the wonderful, but distracting, hubbub of family chaos.

The Ergonomically Correct Scrapbook Space

The type of chair and desk you use and how they are situated will determine how comfortable your scrapbooking hours are, which will in turn impact the number of pages you are able to create in a single crop session. To set up an ergonomic digital crop station make sure to:

- Sit at a height that allows your shoulders to relax when at your keyboard. Your upper arms and forearms should be extended at slightly greater than a right angle. Wrists and hands should extend to the keyboard in a straight line.
- Keep your thighs parallel and your feet flat on the floor (or flat on a foot rest).
- Support your lumbar—purchase a chair with lumbar support or place a small pillow behind your lower back. Try to avoid using chairs with armrests, as they can encourage hunched shoulders or sagging arms. If armrests are unavoidable, make sure they are height adjustable.
- Position the mouse at the same height as your keyboard and within easy reach.

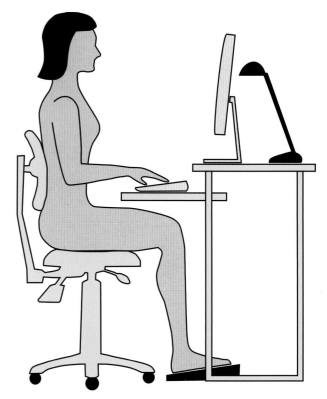

Comfort over the long term is the benefit of an ergonomically correct scrapbook space. Good posture will also keep you working longer without stress.

computer

printer

scanner

My space. My happy space. It's a place where I've spent countless hours designing pages, projects and editing photos. It's a place where all of my digital tools computer, printer, scanner, wacom tablets are kept together, organized and accessible. It's a place that is comfortable and decorated to suit my needs. It's inviting and a place where I want to work and thankfully, it's all mine.

MY HAPPY SPACE

comfy chair

Marla Kress

This artist created a scrapbook page illustrating the attributes of her personal digital scrapbooking crop space. It includes a comfortable chair with an extra cushion for back support, a work surface set to a height that allows her to access her keyboard with the ergonomically-correct hand position, a monitor at eye level, as well as adequate task lighting and storage space.

Make Space for Traditional Supplies

Digital designs can be mixed with traditional scrapbooking supplies for dimension. For example, you may print a digital layout onto archival-quality cardstock and then add fuzzy fibers or silky ribbons, bookplates, beads, bobbles, eyelets, brads, stickers, and more.

Scrapbookers who wish to combine digital and traditional scrapbooking need to organize their cropstation so that it is conducive to both. Efficient use of space is the key: Utilize vertical shelving and organize your supplies so that those you use most are within easy reach. Space permitting, create an L-shaped workstation with your digital set-up on one side and your traditional supplies on the other. Keep wet or messy supplies, such as inks and glitter, a safe distance from your digital equipment. Moist wipes and paper towels are also essential to keep hands and surfaces clean.

Leah Blanco Williams

This page beautifully unites digital and traditional supplies. The photo collage was effortlessly created with image-editing software and then printed on cardstock. Journaling was printed onto a self-adhesive transparency sheet. Leaf clip art was printed onto self-adhesive fabric for easy homemade accents. The traditional elements were mounted on top of the digitally created collage.

Mary-Ann Buchanan

A large-format printer accommodates 12" x 12" paper, which made it possible to easily print this digital layout with edge-to-edge photos.

Digital Bling

Beyond the basics, some scrapbookers enjoy investing in supporting products that expand creative options. Purchase these products online or at your neighborhood electronics store. Products you may want to consider include:

- **Large-format printer:** Digital and traditional scrapbookers appreciate the convenience of printing layouts on 12" x 12" papers. Some printers, such as the Epson Stylus Photo 1280, even offer edge-to-edge printing.
- **Wireless mouse:** A wireless mouse (and other wireless devices) frees you from tethering cords. Follow the manufacturer's instructions for setting up the device.
- **Graphics tablet**: These nifty tablets offer scrapbookers an easy way to add hand drawings, doodles, personal hand-writing, and sketches to layouts. Some feature image-editing capabilities. Disconnect your mouse from your computer to plug in the tablet.
- **Cinema display monitor:** Offering incredible resolution and wide-screen viewing, professional-grade monitors improve the quality and quantity of what you see and are easier on the eyes.

A Girl and Her Machine

Understanding your computer

The computer is the most powerful scrapbooking tool you own, and it pays to spend time with your manuals, identifying its key parts and understanding the way it operates.

Computer Vocabulary

When computer experts speak about their discipline it sounds as if they are conversing in a foreign language. If you want their help, you need to master the basics of tech talk. Here are the most common phrases you, as a digital scrapbook artist, may hear:

- Application: An application is any software program that runs on your computer. Adobe® Photoshop® Elements and Microsoft® Word are both applications.
- Control panel (Mac: System preferences): This is your computer's command center. It allows you to model your computer's behavior to best complement your work flow. Most applications have a Preferences menu that allow you to customize certain features (for example, measuring in inches vs. picas).
- Cross-platform: This is an adjective used to describe any application, font, etc., that can be used on both computer platforms—PC and Mac.

- Hardware: This terms refers to your equipment. A computer, external hard drive, mouse, scanner, etc., are all hardware.
- Hard disk: This is where data, applications, and libraries are stored on your computer. It is also known as the hard drive. On older machines, it may be called the "fixed disk."
- Input device: This term refers to any piece of equipment that allows you to enter information into it, such as a computer or scanner.
- Operating system: This program manages the hardware and software on your computer. On a PC, it's your "Windows" program. If you own a Mac, it's referred to as "OS," which stands for "operating system."
- Output device: This includes any piece of equipment in which data will exit, such as a printer.
- Plug-in: A plug-in (also spelled, "plugin") is a companion application that is designed to work with another application. Photoshop Elements has plug-ins available to perform custom tasks. Many can be downloaded for free or purchased for a nominal fee.
- Software: This term describes any application or plug-in that will be used on hardware.

3 Major Cords

Being able to identify these will help you troubleshoot computer glitches. (Cords pictured in order from left to right.)

- **Ethernet:** This cord looks like a large phone jack. It allows computers to communicate with each other and paves the entrance ramp to the information superhighway.
- **Universal serial bus (USB):** This plug-and-play cord transfers data between your computer and another device such as a digital camera. Most computers have a USB port. A standard USB is limited to transferring only 12 Mbs of data per second. High-speed USB 2.0 can transfer up to 480 Mbs of data per second.
- **FireWire (IEEE 1394 or USB On-the-Go):** More expensive than USB, the speed of data transfer (800 Mbs per second) compensates for the cost. FireWire devices are "hot swappable," meaning you can connect and disconnect while the device and computer are both on (check the instructions for the specific device before you start pulling plugs).

WANTEDWANTED WA {laptop} {laptop} {laptop} {laptop}

SWF sauijhf djka jioj the jkil when the top of the yesterday how to tower other thou goest, I goest, too. Life is such sweet sorrow. Give an inch, take a mile.

SHF (scrap happy female) seeks long-term companion for committed digital scrapping relationship. Must be tidy and considerate, forgiving of mistakes, and willing to spend large amounts of time together. Thriftiness is encouraged. Please enjoy both travel and cozy evenings at home. Must like children, as we will spend much time together with one on my lap. Share your colorful, grungy, traditional and funky sides with me. Serious inquiries only, as I expect to make beautiful memories together that will last for a hundred years or more.

whither thou goest, I goest, too. Life is such sweet sorrow. Give an

laptop *Wanted*

Angelina Schwarz

Digital scrapbookers spend a lot of time with their computers, so it pays to evaluate how well your machine will work for you. Desktop models are excellent, but laptops offer the benefit of anytime-anywhere scrapbooking.

DIGITAL DIVAS KNOW

Using a computer's sleep or standby mode instead of shutting down after each use saves time and energy. This allows the computer to idle, putting the hard drive on "standby," and darkening the monitor. The default amount can be adjusted inside your Control Panel (Mac: System Preferences). Always save work before engaging the sleep mode.

Adobe Photoshop Elements

Many scrapbookers love Photoshop Elements because of its intuitive user interface and powerful image-editing capabilities. Getting acquainted with its features will take the edge off any first-page jitters you might experience when sitting down to digitally scrapbook. Launch your version or the free trial that came with this book and follow along.

The Welcome Screen

When you first launch a software application such as Photoshop Elements, often the first thing you will see is a "Welcome" screen. This screen will give you options for working with the application. For the lessons in this book, select the **Edit menu>Enhance Photos** (Mac: Standard Edit).

A User-friendly Desktop

In the Edit mode, you will see a gray work area where your layout will be located. The Menu Bar and Shortcuts Bar run along the top of your screen. Down the left side, you will see the Toolbox. At the bottom of the desktop is the Photo Bin and on the right side is the Palette Bin.

The Menu Bar

You'll find all of your common tasks, editing functions, and ways in which to organize your work area on the Menu bar. Menus are organized by topic. Take a minute to see what lies under each heading.

The Shortcuts Bar

This bar gives you the most direct way to get a job done. Shortcuts exist for most routine functions, such as opening a file, saving, and printing. These same commands are also found in the Menu bar.

The Options Bar

This bar allows more experienced scrapbookers to customize tool commands via unique settings and options. You'll learn more about the Toolbox in the next chapter (see p. 42 - 43).

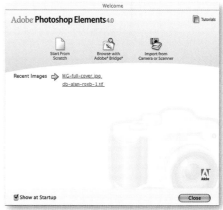

When you launch Photoshop Elements, a welcome screen appears offering a variety of image-editing options. The screen on the left is the PC welcome screen for Elements 5.0; the screen on the right is for Mac, version 4.0. For the lessons in this book opt for "Edit and Enhance Photos."

The Options Bar

The Menu Bar

The Shortcuts Bar

A thorough understanding of your applications desktop is essential for the efficient creation of your scrapbook page.

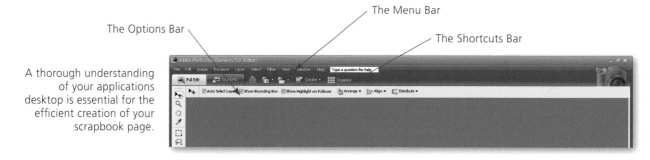

Palettes and Bins

Along the right side of your desktop is a row of tabbed boxes called Palettes. As you digitally alter photos and create digital scrapbook pages, you will use the palettes to manage your workflow. When you open Photoshop Elements for the first time, the Art and Effects and Layers palettes will appear in the Palette Bin. More palette options exist in the Window menu. Palettes can sit independently on your desktop or be stored neatly in the Palette Bin. Palettes can be grouped and docked together as well. If your palette has a More button along the top, click it to find commands specific to each palette.

Photoshop Elements has another type of Bin, the Photo Bin. The Photo Bin will appear along the bottom of the desktop, showing a thumbnail of open images. It's great for toggling between open image files. Through the Photo Bin you can open or close images, duplicate an image, rotate an image, and view file information.

The Window menu, which holds the palette choices is one of your most useful. The palettes shown in the Window menu will appear on your desktop when selected.

The Layers and Undo History palettes are two palettes you should keep in your Palette Bin. The Undo History palette allows you to undo or redo changes you have made to an image. Each time you apply a change to an image, a new state becomes visible in the Undo History palette. To revert to a previous state, simply click on the command you wish to return to. The original state is always displayed at the top of the palette. For more information on Layers, see pp. 46 - 49.

To load individual palettes in the Palette Bin, go to the palette and select "Place in Palette Bin when Closed" from the More drop-down menu; close the window and it will appear in the Palette Bin.

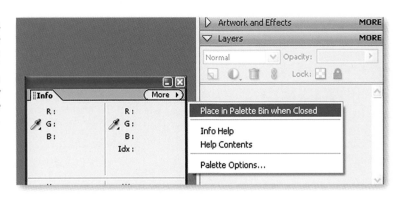

Digital Cameras
Selecting the digital scrapbookers most important accessory

Most digital cameras are lightweight and easy to transport. None require film. However, when shopping for a digital camera, be aware that they do vary widely in cost depending upon the features offered. It is important to understand a bit about the differences between cameras before you can select the camera that best fits your needs.

Camera Specs and Terms

Ads for digital cameras can read like cryptic codes. There are numbers, strange abbreviations, and different types of zooms and features. The information below will help you make sense of the jargon.

Megapixels

The abbreviation "Mpix" stands for megapixels and is followed by a number (3-14). The more megapixels, the higher the image resolution, which is measured in dots per inch (dpi). The higher the resolution, the more information recorded. Below is a chart approximating the number of megapixels needed to make a high-resolution print between 250 and 300 dpi.

4" x 6"	2 megapixels
5" x 7"	3 megapixels
6" x 8"	4 megapixels
8" x 10"	6 megapixels
10" x 14"	8 megapixels
11" x 14"	14 megapixels

Optical Zoom vs. Digital Zoom

Optical zoom lenses produce images with accurate magnification ratios using actual lenses. Digital camera zooms approximate the ratios and perform the zoom with software. Digital zoom can lead to image distortion, reduced detail, and image noise.

Automatic Modes

These special settings (also called program modes) compensate for tough shooting situations, such as low light and fast movement. Common program modes include Portrait and Landscape. Handy bonus modes include Macro for super-close detail, Night Scene to help capture the bright lights of the big city, and Vibration Reduction to lessen the blur caused from camera shake in low-light shooting situations.

Supported Memory

This term refers to the way a camera stores images and to what type of media card (also called a memory stick or memory card) the camera takes. This is the equivalent of film in your digital camera. Common types include CompactFlash, Microdrive, and SecureMedia. Many cameras will support multiple memory formats.

Which Camera Is for You?

Most newer digital cameras have a built-in flash, a variety of automatic exposure modes, and an LCD viewing screen to preview your photos. Beyond these features, digital cameras offer a range of options, especially when it comes to automatic modes, lenses, and sizes.

Digital SLR

The term "SLR" stands for "single lens reflex." SLR cameras have interchangeable lenses, and the image you see in the viewfinder is the actual image reflected from the lens (in non-SLR cameras, the image in the viewfinder is NOT an exact reflection of the image the lens picks up). They also tend to offer the highest image resolution and most creative control. A digital SLR is a good choice for the passionate photographer who is willing to invest in a camera system that will grow with her.

If you have the passion AND the money, the new generation of digital SLR cameras offers the photographer a wealth of features and accessories.

Prosumer

This camera is not quite professional grade but beefier than a top-shelf consumer point-and-shoot model. Prosumers have enviable zoom lenses and tend to offer higher image resolution than point-and-shoot cameras. They are a good choice for the photographer who wants all the bells and whistles without the hassle of interchangeable lenses. Buyer beware: Some prosumer cameras are just as expensive as an SLR but are only slightly more advanced than a point-and-shoot.

Point-and-shoot

The most user-friendly and popular of the digital cameras, point-and-shoots offer a range of resolutions, features, and prices. They almost always have a built-in zoom lens and a variety of automatic modes. These lightweight, affordable cameras tuck easily into a smaller purse or bag.

Compact Point-and-shoot

Also referred to as an ultra-compact point-and-shoot, these little marvels can fit in a shirt pocket and are a good choice for the photographer whose ultimate concern is size and weight. In exchange, you may have to compromise the range of the zoom, the effectiveness of the flash, and the number of features. Compact point-and-shoots tend to be pricier than slightly larger cameras.

Camera Phones

The quality of these devices improves all the time, but your zoom, exposure, flash, and megapixel options are limited. They are great for instant documentation and creating low-resolution images for e-mail and the Web.

The Lens Counts

When you buy a camera, look at the lens. It is the most critical component. Most traditional camera companies, Canon®, Nikon®, Olympus®, etc., match their cameras with their own excellent optics. However, today dozens of companies sell digital cameras. On cameras made by such companies as Kodak®, Panasonic®, Samsung®, Sony®, etc., look at the lens. If you see optics from high-end manufacturers such as Scheider, Leica®, and Carl Zeiss®, it's a keeper.

One of the many advantages to owning a digital SLR is interchangeable lenses. Investing in telephoto, wide-angle, and zoom lenses will help you capture images in a variety of shooting situations.

Jennifer Caputo

Your Scanner
Getting the most from this tool

Scanners are way more than just a copier. They are used by scrapbookers to duplicate and repair price-less photos as well as create custom page accents. The best scanner for you depends upon the type of scrapbooker you are, or hope to become.

Types of Scanners

The flatbed scanner is versatile for crafting and home use. It works much like a photocopier, with a clear glass surface (called a "bed") for scanning photos, papers, and other relatively flat items. If you are serious about photography, you may prefer a film scanner, which is designed to scan slides and 35mm negatives. Some flatbed scanners have adaptors for scanning slides and film.

When it comes to features, higher resolution numbers mean better output. More "bit depth" means better color (this is particularly important if you plan to scan color photos and negatives). Whether the scanner has "optical dpi" or "interpolated dpi" affects color as well as image clarity. Optical dpi will produce a truer image. A higher "scanning resolution" means bigger and better enlargement capabilities. When purchasing a scanner, also take into consideration the speed of scan, maximum document size, and connectivity (FireWire or USB preferred).

Virtually all scanners come with their own scanning software. In addition, some scanners come "bundled" with full versions of image-editing software programs. Bundled software can effectively reduce the actual price of the scanner by hundreds of dollars.

Scanned Images and Resolution

When scanning an image, you must determine the "scanning resolution." Resolution determines how much digital information your scanner records. A higher dpi equals more recorded detail and resolution. An appropriate "scanning resolution" will ensure the resulting image is of the desired quality.

For scanned items intended to be printed, your "final resolution" should be between 240 and 300 dpi. If the item is destined for the Internet or viewing on a computer monitor, 72 to 150 dpi will suffice. Resist the urge to set the scanning resolution higher than necessary. It gobbles up hard drive space and increases printing and data transfer times.

The top image was scanned at a low resolution of 72 dpi. Compared to the bottom 300 dpi scan, it shows a lack of detail, and poor color reproduction.

Do the Math

For the precise scrapbooker, here is the equation for determining scanning resolution

$$\frac{Target\ print\ size}{Original\ print\ size} \times \frac{Desired\ final}{resolution} = \frac{Scanning}{resolution}$$

Example: If you want to enlarge a 4" x 6" photo to 8" x 10" with a final resolution of 300 dpi, your scanning resolution should be 1000 dpi. [8" x 10" (80) ÷ 4" x 6" (24)] × 300 dpi = 1000 dpi

If you want to reduce a 4" x 6" photo to 2" x 3" with a final resolution of 300 dpi, the scanning resolution should be 150 dpi. [2" x 3" (6) ÷ 4" x 6" (24)] x 300 dpi = 75

Note: If you wish to make a same size scan, the scanning resolution and final resolution are the same.

The scanner shown scans both flat items and film, up to large
format, which is film that measures up to 8" x 10".

Square Pegs

While owning a digital camera makes both digital and
traditional scrapbooking easier, it isn't a requirement for
scrapbooking digitally. In fact, many photographers shoot
with both film and digital cameras, enjoying the ease of
digital image editing and the traditional camera's speed and
ability to take multiple frames without delay. Traditional
film cameras can join forces with computer scrapbooking
rather easily. The easiest way to use traditional photos in
digital layouts is to request the photo processor to place the
processed film images on a disk. Or, if you own a scanner,
you may simply choose to scan your processed negatives or
prints. Once images are introduced into your software program in a digital form, you can use them to create all-digital
scrapbook layouts.

Scan-tastic Tips and Tricks

A scanner's greatest strength is its versatility. In the right hands, a scanner can be used to create countless effects for scrapbook pages. As you become familiar with your scanner and your craft, you'll find yourself turning to it more and more frequently.

Care for your scanner by cleaning the glass bed with micro-fiber cloth. Remove dust with canned air or a photo brush. Protect the bed when scanning rough or hard objects with a clear transparency sheet to prevent scratching its surface.

Scan Heritage Photos

Older photos are some of the most precious you own. Before scanners hit the scene, restoration of these images had to be done by a trained professional. But with some know-how, most digital scrapbookers are now able to repair fades, cracks, stains, and yellowing on photos using a scanner with Digital ICE technology. This software identifies and corrects surface defects with the touch of a single button without sacrificing color, vibrancy, or image clarity.

If you have a choice, scan old negatives or slides rather than photos made from them. While photos may have faded over time, negatives and slides are more likely to have maintained their original quality. Be sure your scanner is set to scan the proper media (negative, color negative, slide film, etc.). Increase your scanning resolution to compensate for lower quality, aged images. A resolution of 3000 dpi is optimal for creating an 8" x 10" enlargement from a scanned 35mm negative or transparency (slide).

Clean your prints before scanning by gently buffing them with a dry micro-fiber cloth, canned air, or a photo brush. Clean negatives and transparencies only with compressed air. Do not attempt to clean badly damaged heritage photos (torn, moldy, burnt, or adhered to another surface). Take these fragile treasures to a professional photo restorer.

This artist scanned a heritage photo to use on her digital scrapbook page. Scanners make it easy to copy and share rare heritage photos and heritage scrapbook pages with other family members. Add a quote or journaling digitally to the layout for a truly heartfelt tribute.

Elizabeth Tamanaha

{the sweet life}

FRANCIS & HARRIET

JOY GROWS

NEWLYWEDS

Karen Bowers

Scanning heirloom photos creates a digital image that you can use on a digital or traditional scrapbook page. The now-digital image can be restored with the help of image-editing software. The original photo used for this scrapbook page was faded and yellowed. The artist adjusted the Levels and used Dodge and Burn tools to restore the photo (for more information on using these tools, see pp. 86 - 87).

DIGITAL DIVAS KNOW

Scanned heirloom photos make wonderful gifts for relatives. Burn scanned photos onto discs, then pass them out at the next family gathering. You can scan old family documents, such as wedding licenses and letters, as well.

Scan Ephemera

Scanned ephemera, which is any written or printed material with a short lifespan and includes magazines, trading cards, stamps, postcards, patterns, ticket stubs, greeting cards, bookmarks, and posters, can be used to create unique and meaningful papers and embellishments. When scanning dimensional items, such as a passport or several ticket stubs, place items on the scanning bed and then cover them with a piece of dark cloth to reduce shadows. Print out your scanned ephemera and use it as traditional papers, or simply use it in the digital realm. Traditional scrapbookers can print and cut out scanned items to use as embellishments on theme pages. Mount the printed items with foam adhesive for lifelike dimension.

Mary-Ann Buchanan

This artist created a wonderful background paper and embellishments for her World Traveler layout by scanning stamps, ticket stubs, and a passport. She layered the digital images of the scanned items behind and around her photo and journaling.

Scan Children's Memorabilia

Children come with a lot of memorabilia. Early on, there are birth certificates, announcements, and cards celebrating the new family member. Later, come report cards, spelling tests, finger-painted abstracts, multimedia turkey collages, repurposed paper plates, and first stabs at the Great American Novel. In their natural state, these items are vulnerable to damage. They also require a tremendous amount of storage space within your home. Scanning these treasures reduces them to easily stored images. Incorporate the scanned images onto digital and traditional scrapbook pages.

Angelina Schwarz

A child's poetry and artwork are precious. This artist assured her son's work could be enjoyed for generations to come by scanning it and using the image as part of her digital scrapbook page. A supporting photo showing her son creating the art and an image of his pride in the work balance the layout.

Scan Botanicals

Let nature inspire your creativity. Botanicals have wonderful colors, patterns, and textures. When scanned, they create stunning papers. Mix and match items from nature, including leaves, nuts and berries, flower petals, stems, bark, pollen and seeds, and various grasses. Arrange them decoratively on a transparency sheet to protect the glass bed and scan. You may later decide to digitally alter the colors of your botanical images to work with photos from all seasons.

Erikia Ghumm

On a blustery fall day, this artist stepped outside to collect some fallen leaves, which she scanned to create a custom paper. She also scanned a paint-splattered smock and combined the digital images. Once satisfied with her design, she printed the paper to use as the background for this layout.

More Scanning Ideas

By now, you realize that practically anything can be scanned and digitally manipulated. As you experiment, try scanning these items:

- Photos, negatives, and slides of landscapes, beach scenery, and other venues can be scanned and transformed into patterned paper.
- Found objects, such as bobby pins, coins, sewing supplies, office supplies, kitchen utensils, tools, etc., can be scanned to create papers or individual accents.
- Scanned jewelry is a great way to add shimmer and shine to digital pages. Also, scanning heirloom jewelry is a way to honor your antiques.
- Toys, including blocks, sandbox tools, rattles and teething rings, and even tiny cars can be scanned to create wonderful papers for child-themed pages.

When looking for objects to scan, look beyond the object and pay attention to the texture. These papers were created from scanning everyday items around the house. Interesting textures were sought from a baby sock, the fabric of a baby nursing pillow, sequins from designer wrapping paper, a child's finger painting, and a plastic bag. After the items were scanned, the images were digitally altered to create cool effects. For more information on such techniques, see Chapters 3 and 4.

The Printer
Putting your image on paper

Any scrapbooker, whether digital or traditional, can't go wrong with an inkjet printer. They are available in a variety of sizes, including a few that can print 12" x 12" scrapbook pages. Some models offer a handy transparency or draft setting, which improves the results when printing on vellum or transparencies.

While multi-purpose printers are fine for most printing needs, you'll want to invest in a photo printer with a four- to six-ink printing system if you plan to print photos and scrapbook layouts. A quality printer deserves high quality photo paper that insures the ink doesn't run and feather, which diminishes the quality of the printed image.

True-Color Prints

When what you see on your computer monitor does not look like what prints out, you need to calibrate your monitor to match your printer's color settings. Good color calibration can only be achieved with a quality computer, computer monitor, and printer. Calibration cannot compensate for inferior equipment. Before you begin, look for calibration tips in the owner's manuals for your printer and monitor. Some computer operating systems such as Mac OS X have built-in calibration software to assist you.

The way images look on your monitor is impacted by ambient light, so it's a good idea to calibrate the monitor at the time of day you are most likely to be working. For best results, calibrate in a darkened room. If you need light to work, select a less-lit area and avoid glare on the computer screen. Allow your monitor to warm up at least 15 minutes prior to calibration, and make sure the monitor is in "high-color" mode, or set to 24-bit color. Find these options in your Control Panel (Mac: System Preferences).

Calibration generally requires adjustments to your monitor's brightness and contrast. These controls may be on your monitor itself, or you may have to adjust them via your Control Panel. Once you have located these, print a high-resolution (300 dpi) image onto the photo-quality paper you will be using. (Select a paper you like before you begin the calibration process, as the paper used will affect the color of your print.) Make sure all the print settings are adjusted to your desired paper and resolution. Print an image with a good tonal range and a variety of color, as well as a neutral color (middle gray being the best). Adjust the brightness and contrast of your monitor to correctly match the actual printed photo.

If the colors need further tweaking, repeat this process until you have a match. If you crave even more accurate calibration, additional software and hardware are available to create a color management system for your computer, printer, and digital camera.

The Life Expectancy of a Print

The longevity of a photo, whether a traditional film print or printed digital image, is impacted by the print's chemical make-up and how it is cared for. Studies show that a gently handled and stored traditionally processed photographic print will last 40 to 50 years. Printing your image or scrapbook page on your home inkjet printer may offer the maximum print longevity. Some printer companies boast that prints created using their recommended products, including inks and papers, can last up to 200 years.

The best way to ensure maximum print life, regardless of the source, is to use archival-quality materials that are PVC-, acid-, and lignin-free. Keep photos, negatives, back-up images, and scrapbook albums away from fluctuating temperatures, humidity, and direct sunlight. Wait at least 24 hours for a printed image to dry before placing it in an album. If you live in an area with high humidity, allow a bit longer. For more information about archival concerns, visit www.scrapbookpreservationsociety.com.

DIGITAL DIVAS KNOW

There are many places to get scrapbook pages printed. Just call your neighborhood photo lab, scrapbook store, drug store, or big-box retailer. Chances are, their photo labs will be able to handle any job you throw at them, including printing 12" x 12" layouts. Just take your finished layouts to them on a CD or upload them to their Web site. You can also check out online printers.

Mary-Ann Buchanan, Photo: James Buchanan

This terrific layout was created digitally and then printed onto traditional paper. Because the artist used a quality printer, the digital elements including the layered digital photo mat, digital staples, digital torn paper, and digital stitching, all appear dimensional.

Pick a Pack of Papers

There is a wide world of papers out there on which to print photos, journaling, custom-created digital accents, and completed digital scrapbook pages. High-quality photo paper is available in a variety of finishes for photos and layouts. For a different look, consider printing your photos and layouts on vellum, transparencies, fabric, canvas, ribbon, sheet cork, and specialty papers. Your selected paper can add texture and finish to enhance your photo and page theme.

Vellum and transparencies

Printing on vellum and transparencies is a great way to create a custom overlay, compensate for a slightly blurry photo, or create a dreamy effect. If your inkjet printer has a "transparency" or "draft" setting (located in your printing preferences), selecting it will cause your printer to use less ink on these nonporous materials. If your printer does not have a special transparency selection, set the ink with a heat gun (be very careful not to melt your transparency). Vellums and transparencies print beautifully on laserjet printers, but when printing transparencies, use only those created specifically for laserjet printers. Inkjet transparencies melt in a laserjet printer. When printing on a transparency, double-print the image or text to ensure ink saturation.

Lighter weight vellums generally produce better results than heavier stocks. But vellum is a bit fragile. It creases and is easily soiled, so handle it with care. Trim vellum with a craft knife and metal-edge ruler rather than scissors.

Specialty papers

A paper's thickness is measured by weight, and most printers can handle paper with up to a 110-lb weight. Textured and natural papers often are of heavier weights than normal printer paper. For best results, use a mid-weight paper (approximately 65 lbs). Avoid printing on papers with a specialty finish and on synthetic papers. Remember that images and text printed on heavyweight and highly textured papers appear less defined than those printed on glossier surfaces.

Fabric and ribbon

Use an inkjet printer when printing on fabric; a laserjet printer can become too hot. Fabric sheets must be "stabilized" or they will jam the printer. Pre-stabilized fabric sheets are available for scrapbooking and can be found online and at your local hobby or scrapbook store. You can also stabilize fabric with an iron-on fabric stabilizer. Or iron the back side of the fabric to the shiny side of freezer paper. Canvas, muslin, and cotton work best. Check the remnant bins at fabric stores for bargain buys.

When printing on fabric, cut stabilized fabric slightly smaller than 8½" x 11". Trim errant strings that might catch in your printer's moving parts. Check your printer's Preferences menu for potential adjustments for thicker media and to use as much ink as possible. Monitor the fabric as it feeds through the printer to prevent curling. Once the ink is dry, set it by placing a piece of parchment paper on your stabilized fabric and ironing.

To print on ribbon, use a word-processing program to type text into a new document. Print the document. Using a piece of double-sided tape, adhere the ribbon over the top of the printed text. Re-insert the paper into the printer and print again. Twill or twill tape works best, but satin ribbon can be printed upon as well. If you can't put ribbon in your printer, remember you can always scan the ribbon and place text on top of it in a digital layout.

DIGITAL DIVAS KNOW

Check the printer's owner's manual before printing on specialty media. Your manual will detail the type, size, and thickness of the media it can handle. To save money, always print a test copy on regular paper before committing to your specialty media. Print from the manual print tray when using specialty media to prevent jams. Finally, if printing multiple copies of one image, print each copy individually to ensure correct printing each time.

Printing photos on canvas adds texture and warmth. Canvas can be purchased at art-supply and hobby stores. Once the photos have been printed, use a needle to pull out the string along the edges to fray them.

Transparencies allow the printed photo to retain all of its definition while giving the artist creative layering options. Here, the photo is layered over a strip of patterned paper.

Michelle Pesce

Michelle Pesce

Printing on textured cardstock is an affordable option for photo-printing. Plus, the slight texture can enhance a photo.

Michelle Pesce

Organizing Digital Files
Cataloging your prolific creativity

Are digital files littering your desktop, rendering the hard drive unnavigable, transforming folders into riddles of numbered file names? It is time to organize. Image-organization software is made specifically to help you get a handle on your digital library. Image-editing software often features a storage and organization system and most digital cameras come bundled with image-organization software as well. You'll also want a system for backing up your files in case disaster strikes, erasing your images from your computer's storage space.

File-naming Basics

The names originally given to files by your system (ex: IMG_007.jpg) won't help you locate a specific image in the future. So take the time to rename your files before storing them. The key to successful file naming is consistency and simplicity. Begin file names with the date, followed by the theme, and then add a subtopic if you can. For example, the photo below is saved with the file name, "0906_ACL_jaime.jpg"; it tells the owner that this photo of Jaime was taken in September 2006 at the Austin City Limits festival. Files can also be named with just the date and event or date and photo subject's name. Save space by using numerals for the month and year (example: 1207 instead of December 2007). Group themed images into their own folders. Place any finished digital layouts utilizing the images into the same folder.

Immaculately Organized Photos

Ambitious scrapbookers who take many photos depend upon their software for organization. Photoshop Elements 5.0, for example, offers the Organizer (Mac: Adobe Bridge) that organizes and labels image files. Files can be tagged with keywords corresponding to names, places, or events. Clicking on a tag displays related images. By grouping images into collections with your organization software, you can easily find current and previously saved versions of photos and layout projects.

Save new files and altered originals using Save As (under the File menu), which allows you to alter the file name, file type, and location. You can also choose to add your finished layouts or photos to the Elements Organizer.

Label and sort your scrapbook pages as well as your photos
with Photoshop Elements Organizer.

Back Up Your Images

Accidents happen. Therefore, backing up your images is a
good idea. Make a commitment to invest in updating your
technology as times change. Today's cutting-edge methods
of preserving memories will become outdated, and it is up
to you to change with the times to protect your memories.

- The simplest way is to store a second set of your favorite
  photos and all finished layouts on a CD. If protected from
  dust, scratches, direct sunlight, heat, and humidity, better
  quality CDs can last more than 100 years.

- Online photo-printing services also offer image storage.
  It's free, occupies no personal space or hard drive space,
  and allows select others to view the images and even
  order their own prints.

- For a minimal investment you can purchase a separate
  compact hard drive that provides tremendous space for
  storing digital photos, layouts, music, and personal
  documents. Many external hard drives come with software that automatically will back up your data.

Susan Weinroth

Gussy up your CD storage
boxes or repurpose an old
milk crate to house your
digital depot. Look for
storage boxes at your local
discount store.

Best friends

Jessica and Michaela met in kindergarten and became instant best friends. They always get along and bring out the best in each other.

Susha Roberts

Digital Layouts 101

To become a confident digital scrapbooker, you must first master the basics before moving on to more exciting challenges. This chapter provides you with the vital information you need in order to create the digital layout of your dreams, all in an easy-to-follow, step-by-step format. You will also find insider advice about alternative options for carrying out commands in this "more than one way to skin a cat" realm of digital scrapbooking, ways to avoid digital disasters, and handy digital scrapbooking terms.

The chapter is illustrated with terrific digital artwork created by the best artists in the scrapbooking world. As you master the basics of creating digital layouts, you'll find yourself evaluating and appreciating the design magic these digital savants weave in a way you never thought possible. With this knockout punch of basics, design tips, and sage advice under your belt, you'll soon (very soon) be following in the footsteps of the masters of digital design.

Page-Building Basics
A step-by-step guide to creating your first digital layout

You are five easy lessons away from creating your first digital scrapbooking page. Once you master these basic skills, you're free to move about the world of digital image manipulation and graphic design with confidence.

Our advice is to follow through, step-by-step, until you feel that you've "got it." Then, dog-ear this section to use as a quick reference for your many solo voyages through digital scrapbooking.

Your Basic Tools

On the left side of the desktop of Photoshop Elements, you will find the Toolbox (if you don't see it, go to the Window drop-down menu and choose Tools). These tools allow you to select and alter layers and individual items on your canvas. Spend some time familiarizing yourself with these handy guys. Select a tool with the mouse. When you move the cursor to the document window, the tool's icon will become visible. Hold down the tool button on the Toolbox to reveal hidden tools, or find them on the Options bar. If you need more help with a tool, click on it and linger over it. The tool's name and its keyboard shortcut will appear. Click on the tool name and the Adobe Help Center will open with an explanation of what it is and how to use it.

Zoom (Z) Just click on the image or canvas to zoom in (magnified view) or out (smaller view). Select the magnifying lens with a plus (+) to zoom in and a minus (-) to zoom out. If you are using another tool, you can zoom in and out with a keyboard shortcut: Hold down the Control key (Mac: Cmd) and push the (+) to zoom in or the (-) to zoom out.

Eyedropper (I) Use to sample colors from one part of an image to fill in other areas. This is an excellent way to match elements to photographs on your page. The sampled color appears in the Foreground Color box at the bottom of the Toolbox.

| Rectangular Marquee Tool | M |
| Elliptical Marquee Tool | M |

Rectangular Marquee (M) Use this tool to make a rectangular selection on your image. Once your area is selected, you can perform a variety of alterations, including delete. This is an excellent tool for cropping your photos without cropping the canvas (hidden: Elliptical Marquee to make circular and oval selections).

Lasso (L) Use this tool to make a freehand selection around part of an image. Use this tool to select a detail from an image to use as an embellishment on your page. Once the area is selected, cut and paste the extracted item onto a new layer on your layout. You can also select the inverse and delete everything around the selection (hidden: Polygonal Lasso for making selections on objects with horizontal and vertical lines; Magnetic Lasso for making selections to objects with well-defined edges).

Magic Wand (W) Select areas of an image by selecting areas of similar color with this tool. In the Options bar, set Tolerance to include more or less information (a higher Tolerance number means more information will be included). This tool is excellent for selecting areas to delete when you want to extract a portion of an image from the background.

Selection Brush (A) This tool allows you to make selections with a brush tip rather than a freehand Lasso. If you find yourself feeling clumsy with the Selection Brush, try the Magic Selection Brush (hidden), which works on the same principle as the Magic Wand. It's not very precise for items that blend into the background, but it's good for solid-colored objects and items that contrast with the background.

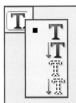

Horizontal Type (T) This tool allows typing of text onto an image or canvas. Get to know this tool—you'll use it for all of your titles and journaling (hidden: Vertical Type; Horizontal and Vertical Type Mask tools for creating selections in text shapes, which act like a digital die-cutting machine, allowing you to cut letter shapes from digital patterned paper and photos).

Crop (C) To delete unwanted information from an individual photo that is not yet placed in a document, use this tool. Remember, this tool crops the entire document (or canvas) and not just a selected photo or digital paper. Crop photos before placing them in your document. To trim a photo or paper in a pre-existing layout, use the Rectangular Marquee tool.

Cookie Cutter (Q) Quickly crop your photos in a variety of resizable shapes. Choose shapes in the Options bar.

Straighten Tool (P) This tool easily corrects crooked images, such as an off-kilter city skyline or tilting building.

Red-eye Removal (Y) Removes red-eye from people and animals. Drag it over the eye you want to fix, and it automatically corrects the color.

Healing Brush (J) This easily corrects flaws or removes unwanted items over a large area (hidden: Spot Healing Brush for smaller blemishes).

Clone Stamp (S) For retouching, it will copy an area of an image to be reapplied, or stamped, onto another area (hidden: Pattern Stamp for retouching with a selected pattern). This is another great tool for airbrushing blemishes and duplicating detail elements. With the level of control it allows, you can get professional results.

Eraser (E) Use this tool to erase parts of an image. When you erase on a layer, the deleted areas become transparent, allowing the background to show through. Use the Eraser to knock out elements or create rough edges on photos and papers (hidden: Background Eraser for erasing on the Background layer).

Brush (B) Use to paint an image with foreground color, custom color page elements, or create original artwork on your page (hidden: Color Replacement tool for recoloring a page element; Impressionist Brush gives photos a painterly effect; Pencil tool to freehand draw lines to accent your page).

Paint Bucket (K) Use to fill an enclosed area with color or fill boxes and shapes with color to match your page.

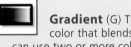

Gradient (G) This fills a selected area with color that blends from one hue to another; you can use two or more colors and blend in a variety of angles and shapes. Great for backgrounds and mats.

Shape Selection (U) Hidden under this arrow are the Rectangle, Rounded Rectangle, Ellipsis (circles), Polygon, Line, and Custom Shape tools. Use these tools for fun journaling blocks and more.

Sharpen (R) This tool increases the edge definition of an image, allowing you to control the amount of sharpness and retouch specific areas to avoid the graininess found in over-sharpened photos. Drag it over soft edges to subtly add contrast and sharpen the look of your photos (hidden: Smudge for the look of a finger painting; Blur for blurring just part of an image—it's great for dulling distracting elements or creating movement).

Sponge (O) This tool subtly changes color saturation to make a selected area more vibrant (hidden: Dodge, to add brightness and to sharpen detail in underexposed areas; Burn, to emphasize items lost in overexposed areas of an image).

Foreground Color Click this to open the Color Picker to choose alternate colors for the foreground. Just under it is Background Color. Click on the small black-and-white box to reset the default foreground and background colors to black and white, respectively. Click on the arrows to switch foreground and background colors. If you want to extract elements on a white page, don't forget to set the background color to white before you hit Delete or use the Eraser tool.

Lesson 1: Create Your Canvas

The steps to building your digital layout resemble the steps taken to create a paper layout. A paper layout, from the ground up, has layers of elements, and so does a digital layout. But for a digital layout, your mouse pointer and image-editing tools become extensions of your hands, handling, moving, and further manipulating the digital elements.

Over the next few pages, you will find detailed instructions. In the back of the book you will find a CD. On the CD there are two trial versions of Adobe Photoshop Elements, one for PC and one for Mac. The basic instructional text in this book is illustrated using Adobe Photoshop Elements 5.0. (If you are using a Mac or an earlier version of Elements, there may be subtle differences in instructions. Please refer to your Elements owner's manual.) Also on the CD are four digital page kits created exclusively for this book by scrapbooking's hottest designers. Download the kits from the CD to your computer to re-create many of the book's projects with your own photos and journaling or to use for completely original designs.

Every scrapbook page must have a foundation on which to blossom, so to begin creating a digital layout, you must first create the canvas. To do this you must determine what size your scrapbook page will be, how many pages (will you create a single- or double-page layout?), and whether or not the layout is destined for printing.

If you plan to print your pages, you'll want to create layouts in a size that your printer can handle. Standard scrapbook page sizes are 12" x 12", 8½" x 11", 8" x 8", and 6" x 6". Most digital scrapbookers favor an 8" x 8" format—a very manageable size that, over time, will save hard-drive space.

When opening a new document, the "New" dialog box gives you a choice of color modes. Color modes determine how your images will look on the monitor and in print. Photoshop Elements offers four modes: RGB, Grayscale, Bitmap, and Indexed. RGB, an acronym for "red, green, blue," creates all of the possible color combinations in your image. RGB is the mode of choice, as it is the default color mode in Photoshop Elements. Unless specified, all step-by-step projects in this book will utilize RGB mode.

Note:

All the elements used in the lessons can be found on the Scrapbooking Digitally CD in the folder titled "Lesson."

Step 1

Launch your software. Select **File>New>Blank File**. A dialog box will appear, giving you the option to name your layout and determine the dimensions of the canvas (make sure "inches" is selected; for this lesson, the canvas should be 8" x 8"). You also will have resolution and color choices. If you are planning to print, set the resolution for 300 dpi and the color to RGB.

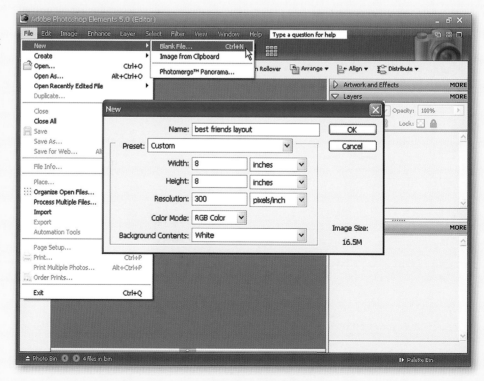

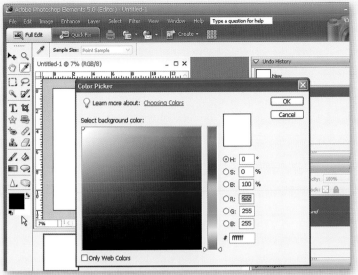

Step 2

To choose a color for the Background layer, click the Background color icon on the Toolbox (the Foreground and Background color icons overlap each other; the default setting positions the Foreground icon on top). In the dialog box, select the desired color in the vertical bar and a block of gradient color will appear. Click on a shade, tone, or tint in the color sampling area to select it for the background; click OK. Using the Paint Bucket tool, click on the background to fill it with color. For this lesson, the Background layer has been left white.

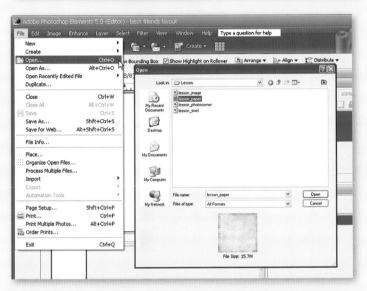

Step 3

Add a digital patterned paper from the kit CD. Choose **File>Open>CD>Lesson>lesson_paper**. Click Open.

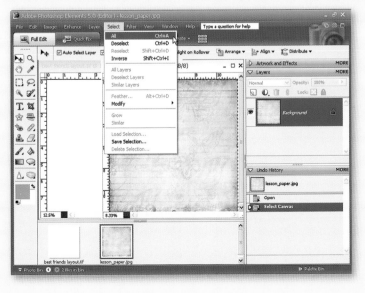

Step 4

The "lesson_paper" file will appear in an active window and in the Photo Bin. Choose **Select menu>All** to select the entire paper. (If you are using Elements 5.0, you can click and drag the paper to your layout file; hold down the Shift key while you drag and Elements 5.0 will center and resize your paper proportionately. Skip steps 5-8.)

Step 5

To copy the selected patterned paper, choose **File menu>Copy**.

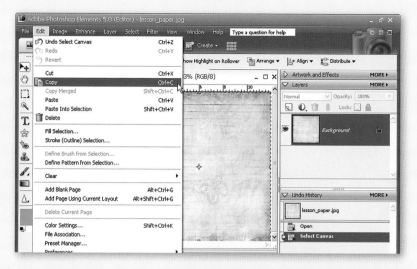

Step 6

Go to the Photo Bin, click on the layout document, and it will appear in the active window. Choose **Edit menu>Paste** to import the copied patterned paper to the document.

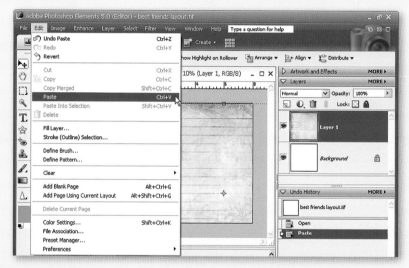

Step 7

If your layout is smaller than 12" x 12", the patterned paper will be larger than the canvas. To resize the patterned paper, select the Move tool from the Toolbox. A bounding box will appear with squares on the corners and sides. Drag the corner to resize the paper. Click the green checkmark to confirm.

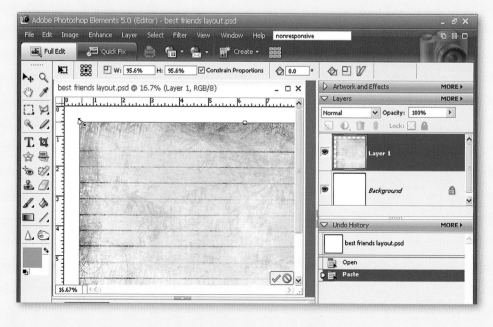

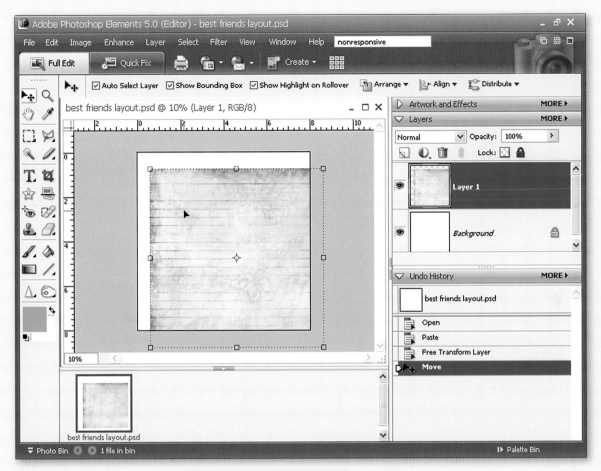

Step 8

To reposition the resized patterned paper on the layout, position the Move tool inside the bounding box (a dark arrow will appear). Drag the patterned paper to its desired location; click the green checkmark to confirm. For this lesson, the paper should fill the entire layout canvas.

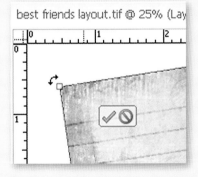

If you want to rotate an item, hover the Move tool near a corner square of an element and a curved, double-arrow will appear. Drag the arrow left or right and click the green checkmark to confirm.

Quick Guide: Creating Your Canvas

- Launch software.
- Choose **File menu>New>Blank File.** The keyboard shortcut is Ctrl-N (Mac: Cmd-N).
- Name the file.
- Set the dimensions.

- Set the resolution (300 dpi for best print quality).
- Set the color mode (RGB preferred).
- Click the Foreground color icon in the Toolbox to select a color (the default color is white); choose the Paint Bucket and click on the canvas to apply color.

The Power of Layers

Before adding anything else to the layout, it is essential to understand layers. Layers make it possible to change, alter, and rearrange elements individually. With layers, you can add elements to a photo without altering the original file (for example, if you want to add text to an image, you create a text layer on top of a photo layer without affecting the original image). Layers also allow for incredible image manipulation effects, image collage, and photo retouching. These advanced techniques will be covered in subsequent chapters.

To understand how layers work, you should think of your digital layouts not as flat, two-dimensional documents but as a digital document consisting of multiple strata (layers)—a background layer, a photo layer, a text layer, etc. They are like separate transparent sheets that page elements rest upon; they are transparent except where images, text, elements, colors, textures, and patterns appear.

Before starting to work with layers, there are a few important aspects you should remember. You can edit only one layer at a time. Layers increase the size of your document, so delete unwanted layers when working. Also, you should merge layers together when you are completely satisfied with your work to reduce document size. The merging together of all layers is called "flattening."

Create a New Layer

Every image opened and every new document created in Photoshop Elements exists on a default layer called the Background. This layer is locked and cannot be edited. Even if you wish to work inside only one layer, you must duplicate or unlock the background layer. For more complex operations, use an adjustment layer (this leaves the original unaltered).

First, identify the Layers palette. When Photoshop Elements is launched for the first time, it will appear on the right side of the screen. If the Layers palette does not appear when you open a new document, go to the Window drop-down menu and choose Layers. Inside the Layers palette you can create, rename, select, and manipulate layers; the layers will appear in the order in which they are created (Background is at the bottom and subsequent new layers are created above it). You also can manually rearrange the layers (see p. 51). This is important—the order in which your layers are stacked will affect the resulting image. Images in the top layers will "cover" elements in layers below them.

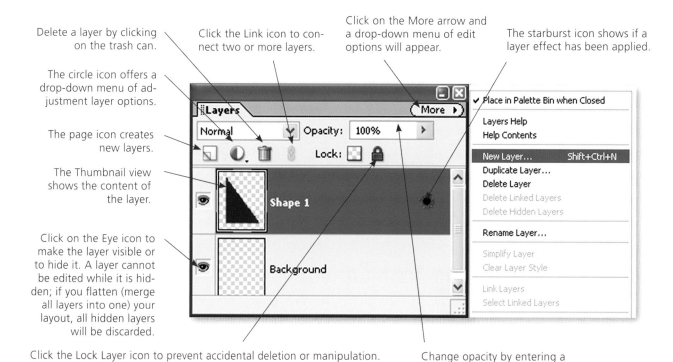

Delete a layer by clicking on the trash can.

Click the Link icon to connect two or more layers.

Click on the More arrow and a drop-down menu of edit options will appear.

The starburst icon shows if a layer effect has been applied.

The circle icon offers a drop-down menu of adjustment layer options.

The page icon creates new layers.

The Thumbnail view shows the content of the layer.

Click on the Eye icon to make the layer visible or to hide it. A layer cannot be edited while it is hidden; if you flatten (merge all layers into one) your layout, all hidden layers will be discarded.

Click the Lock Layer icon to prevent accidental deletion or manipulation. Next to the Lock Layer icon is the checkerboard Lock Transparent Pixels icon. This prevents manipulation of only transparent areas on a layer.

Change opacity by entering a number or clicking on the arrow for an adjustable slider.

Types of Layers

These different types of layers are the source of many different kinds of special effects.

Aside from the Background layer, the type of layer created is dependent on the content of the layer. For example, if you select the Type tool, a Type layer will automatically be created once you begin typing. New Fill and Adjustment layers (see p. 93) must be selected from the More menu in the Layers palette.

- **Background layer:** This is the bottom layer of any layered layout or image. Because it contains the original data of an image, it is always locked; to manipulate the content on this layer, choose **Layers palette>More>Duplicate Layer** or right-click on the Background layer and choose Layer from Background to transform the Background to an ordinary layer.
- **Ordinary layer:** These are image layers and your most basic type of layer. You use them to work on photos. They are pixel-based.
- **Fill layer:** These are color layers, containing either gradient color, solid color, or a pattern.
- **Adjustment layer:** As you advance in image manipulation, you'll love these layers for their refinement capabilities. Deft use of these layers results in expert color, brightness, and saturation adjustment without permanently affecting the original image.
- **Type or Shape layers:** With these layers, you can use vector graphics to create text and shapes (vector graphics are created from the actual lines and curves of defined shapes instead of pixels, which are square).

Shown above is the Layer menu with the New Adjustment Layer selected.

Quick Guide: Working With Layers

Creating a new layer
- Do one of the following:
  1. Choose **Layer menu>New>Layer**.
  2. Choose **Layers palette>More>New Layer**.
  3. Use the keyboard shortcut **Shift-Ctrl-N** (Mac: Shift-Cmd-N).
  4. Click on the New Layer icon in the Layers palette.

- In the dialog box that appears, choose to do the following (these options can also be adjusted later):
  1. Rename the layer.
  2. Choose a blending mode.
  3. Determine the level of opacity.

Selecting a layer
- Do one of the following:
  1. On the Layers palette, click the layer name to activate the layer.
  2. Hover your mouse over the desired object or image (a blue box will tell you what item you are over). Click and the layer will be selected.

Deleting a layer
- Select the desired layer and do one of the following:
  1. Choose **Layers palette>More>Delete Layer**.
  2. Click the Trash icon on the Layers palette and then click "Yes."
  3. Drag the layer into the Trash icon on the Layers palette.

Manage Layers

As you add layers, you may wish to rearrange them to achieve a specific visual effect or place one element in front of another. This can be done by selecting the layer(s) in the Layers palette and moving it/them into desired sequential order. To move a layer, click its name and hold the mouse button while you drag the layer to the desired location (a fist will appear while you are dragging the layer).

It is also a good idea to rename the layers. Working on images that utilize more than a few layers can get confusing if all of the layers are simply called "Layer 1," "Layer 2," etc. Rename image or fill layers with basic descriptives, such as "kid photo" or "gradient layer"; text layers are named by what you have typed. To rename a layer, double click on it and type a new name.

You can edit only one layer at a time. A layer that is being edited is called the "active" layer. It will appear blue inside the Layers palette. To activate a layer, simply click on its name in the Layers palette. If you have several layers to which you wish to apply the same changes, you can link those layers. Hold down the Ctrl key (Mac: Cmd) and click on the desired layers; click the Link icon (it looks like a chain link) in the Layers palette. To unlink layers, click the Link icon again.

If you wish to prevent further changes on a layer, you can "lock" it. A locked layer will feature a padlock icon next to its name. You can still move locked layers (except for the Background). To lock a layer, select it and click either the Lock Layer icon (padlock) to lock the entire layer or the Lock Transparent Pixels icon (checkerboard) to lock only the transparent areas of the layer. Click either icon again to unlock.

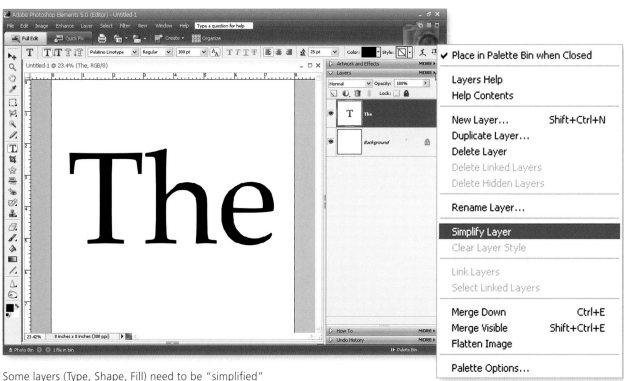

Some layers (Type, Shape, Fill) need to be "simplified" before you can apply filters or use brush tools on them. To simplify a layer, select the desired layer and choose **Layers palette>More>Simplify Layer**. Once a type or shape layer is simplified, you cannot use the type- or shape-editing options.

DIGITAL DIVAS KNOW

When working on an original image, you should make a duplicate layer on which to apply changes. That way you always have a point of reference, and if you go too far you can start over on an unaltered original image.

Use Layers to Create Illusions

By adjusting the blending modes and the opacity of layered images, multidimensional effects, such as transparent text or photo composites, can be created. To utilize these features look for blending modes and opacity on top of the Layers palette.

- **Blending modes:** These blend the colors and tonal values of two stacked layers. Various blending modes result in different effects.
- **Opacity:** Adjust the slider to control the opaqueness of a layer (if the opacity is 100 percent, the layer is totally opaque, hiding the layers beneath).

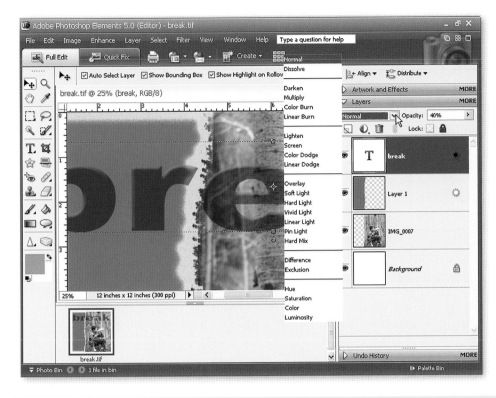

The opacity of the Type layer was reduced to make this word appear transparent. Blending modes can be selected from the drop-down menu. The blending mode for these letters was set to "difference," making them look like clear "gel" stickers.

Quick Guide: Managing Layers

Showing/hiding a layer
- To hide the layer, click the Eye icon on the Layers palette. Hidden layers will not be included when you merge layers or flatten your document.
- Reclick to make the eye reappear and the layer visible again on the desktop.

Changing the order of the layers
- Select the layer you wish to move.
- Drag the layer (a Fist icon will appear) to the desired position on the Layers palette (a thick line will signal successful repositioning).
- Release the mouse when the layer is repositioned.

Linking layers (to make changes affect multiple layers)
- Click on a layer. Add layers to link by holding down the Ctrl key (Mac: Cmd) and clicking those as well.
- Click on the Link icon. To unlink, reclick the Link icon.

Merging layers
Use the merge function if you want to decrease your file size. Note: If you choose to merge layers with type, be aware that you will no longer be able to edit the text.
- Click on a layer. Select additional layers by holding down the Ctrl key (Mac: Cmd) and choosing **Layers palette >More>Merge Layers**.
- The merged layer will appear in the position of the topmost layer you have selected.
- Hide layers you don't want to merge, then choose **Layers palette>More>Select Merge Visible**.

Locking and unlocking layers
- Select desired layers and click the desired Lock icon: Lock All icon (padlock) to lock the entire layer or Lock Transparent Pixels icon (checkerboard) to lock only the transparent areas of the layer.
- To unlock layers, select them, and reclick the Lock icon.

Lesson 2: Place and Size Photos

Once the canvas has been created, photos can be added. Introducing photos to a digital layout is called "importing." Photos can be imported from your hard drive, digital camera, scanner, CD/DVD, flash drive, and digital video camera. If importing images from your digital camera or other devices, check the owner's manual for instructions.

Photos also can be imported from the desktop or a photo's respective folder. Photoshop Elements 5.0 features the Photo Bin. This bin sits at the bottom of the screen and houses all of the photos that you've opened while working in the program. Select a photo from the bin and drag-and-drop it onto your canvas; otherwise, you can copy and paste images onto your canvas.

Step 1

Determine the images you wish to use on the page and open them by selecting **File menu>Open**. A dialog box will appear; browse to locate your desired image (for this lesson, go to **CD>Lesson>lesson_ image**). When you've located the image, click **Open**. The image will appear in an active window and also in the Photo Bin.

Step 2

Choose **Select menu>All** to select the entire image and then choose **Edit menu>Copy** to copy.

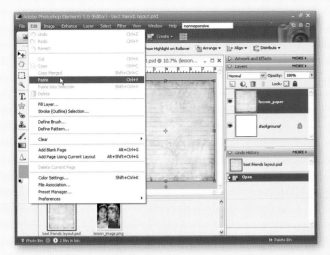

Step 3

Choose **Edit menu>Paste** to insert the image. The image will be placed on a layer directly above the current layer. Photoshop Elements 5.0 will allow you to drag the image directly from the Photo Bin onto your layout.

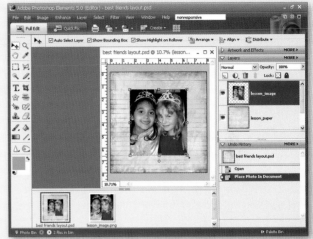

Step 4

Select the Move tool from the Toolbox and a bounding box (a line with little squares on the sides and corners) will appear around the image. Click and drag on a corner or side square to resize.

Step 5

To reposition the resized image on the layout, position the Move tool inside the bounding box (a dark arrow will appear). Drag the image to its desired location. Click on the green checkmark to implement your changes.

Quick Guide: Adding and Resizing an Image

- Open the Image you wish to use (**File menu> Open> IMAGE NAME>click Open**).
- The image will appear in an active window. Choose **Select menu>All** to select the entire image and then **Edit menu>Copy**.
- Select your layout to make it active. Choose **Edit menu>Paste** to insert the image.

- To resize the image, use the Move tool to grab a square in the bounding box and drag to the desired size.
- To rotate the image, hover the Move tool over a corner of the image and a curved, double-arrow will appear: drag left or right to rotate (hold down the Shift key to rotate in 15-degree increments).

Lesson 3: Add and Format Text

Photos are rarely at home on a scrapbook page without a few text details. Take some time to gather your thoughts to create a compelling title and journaling that brims with detail. Be sure you have enough space for your powerful words (although, the nice thing about digital is that you can readjust elements if you find you've miscalculated the space needed).

When you add type to a layout using Photoshop Elements, it exists on its own layer and, therefore, can be manipulated just like any other layer (remember, to apply most special effects and painting, you will have to simplify the layer; refer to p. 50 for instructions). You can play with the opacity and blending modes and edit text at will. Move it, layer it, and combine it with images. Note that text can only be added to documents created in the RGB and grayscale color modes.

Select the Type tool, and the Options bar will list fonts and allow you to adjust the text size. To select fonts, highlight text with the cursor and scroll through fonts on the Options bar. The text automatically changes to the font selected in the Options bar. Line spacing, or leading, can be changed from the Options bar as well. Select the lines of text you wish to change and choose a value from the line-spacing menu, or enter a new value into the box.

If your final text is larger than 14 points in size you'll want to Anti-alias it. Otherwise the text will appear jagged. (If you Anti-alias 14-point and smaller type, it will appear blurred.) To Anti-alias your text, select the type layer in the Layers palette and click the Anti-alias icon on the Options bar, or choose **Layer menu>Type>Anti-alias On**. For much more information about working with text on digital scrapbook pages, see Chapter 4, Letter-Perfect Text (pp. 110 - 145).

Step 1

Select the Type tool. In the Options bar, select the font and font size. Click on the canvas in the desired text location; a new layer will automatically appear when you start to type your title.

Step 2

To make changes to the font or text size, select the text layer you wish to alter. Select the text to change (click and drag the cursor over the text; it will appear "highlighted"). Apply color through the Options bar. It offers a drop-down menu of color choices; if you click on the colored box, the Color Picker will appear so you can create custom colors (see p. 150 for more info). You can also match your text color to elements on your layout using the Eyedropper tool. For this layout, the opacity (in the Layers palette) was changed to 60 percent for the word "Best"; the colored text looks lighter, and the background can now be seen through the word.

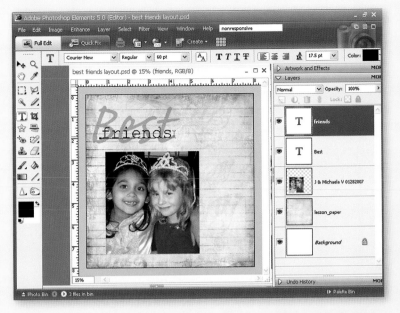

Step 3

To add the second word to the title, select the Type tool again and customize it as desired in the Options bar. Click on the document and another text layer will be created. Resize and reposition as desired using the Move tool (see p. 53 for instructions).

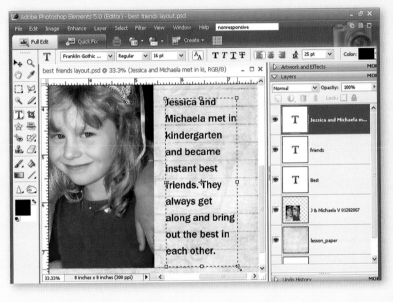

Step 4

When finished with the title, select the Type tool again to add your journaling. To create a block of text, drag the Type tool across the canvas and a bounding box will appear. Choose left-, center- or right-justify in the Options bar. Type your text in the box and the text will automatically wrap.

Grab and drag the side or corner squares to resize the text box as needed. The box can also be rotated and repositioned (see p. 53 for instructions).

Quick Guide: Adding and Formatting Text

Adding text
- Select the Type tool. Click inside document; a new layer will automatically be created. Type desired text.

Editing text
- Activate desired Type layer from the Layers palette.
- Highlight and edit text just as you would in any word-processing program.
- When finished, click anywhere on the canvas or click the green checkmark in the Options bar to accept changes.

Creating text blocks
- To create blocks of text that automatically wrap, select the Type tool and drag a box onto your layout. Once the box is created, select the desired justification from the Options bar, and type text. Change the size of the text box by dragging the squares on the bounding box.

Applying color to text
- Click on the Text layer you wish to alter.
- Select the text in that layer you wish to color.
- Color the text using the Color Picker in the Options bar.

Lesson 4: Add Embellishments

Page embellishments are the perfect way to spice up a scrapbook layout. Digital scrapbookers can use digital stickers, brads, eyelets, beads, baubles, chipboard letters and shapes, epoxy accents, metal charms, and more. They achieve the look of stamping, distressing, and painting elements on a layout with the touch of a button and a little optimizing. Digital scrapbookers who crave a more hands-on approach can create their own custom digital accents, but when you are just getting started, it is easiest to embellish your layout by dragging and dropping (or copying and pasting) premade elements onto your page.

Premade digital accents work just like image files. You can alter and adjust them just like you would an image. If you need to resize an accent, follow the same steps as you would to resize a photo.

Step 1

Determine the embellishments you wish to use on the page and open them by selecting **File menu>Open**. A dialog box will appear; browse to locate your desired image (for this lesson, go to **CD>Lesson>lesson_swirl**); click Open. The embellishment will appear in an active window and in the Photo Bin. Choose **Select menu>All** and then **Edit menu>Copy**. (Elements 5.0 will allow you to drag and drop the embellishments from its file to your layout document; 5.0 users, skip step 2.)

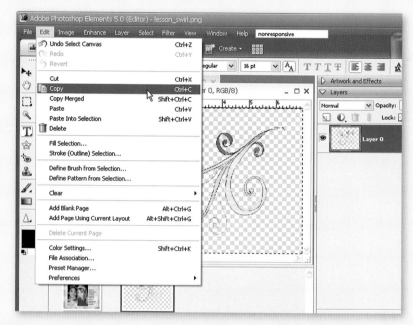

Step 2

Go to the Photo Bin and activate your layout document. Choose **Edit menu>Paste** and the embellishment will be placed on a layer directly above the current layer.

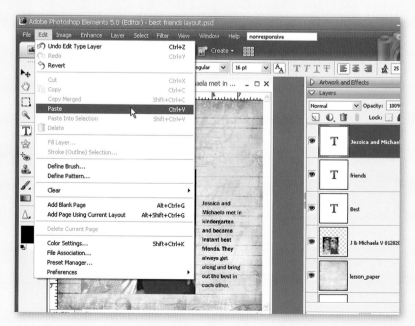

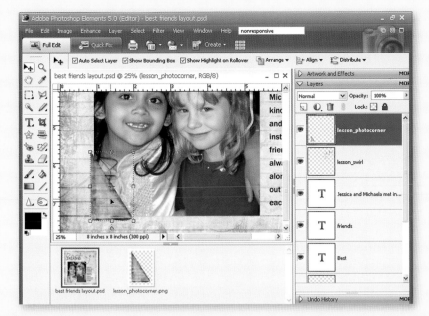

Step 3

Select the Move tool from the Toolbox and a bounding box will appear around the embellishment. Grab a corner or side square to resize.

To rotate, hover your Move tool over a corner and a curved, double-arrow will appear; drag left or right to rotate. If you hold the Shift key while rotating, the embellishment will rotate in 15-degree increments. Click on the green checkmark to implement your changes.

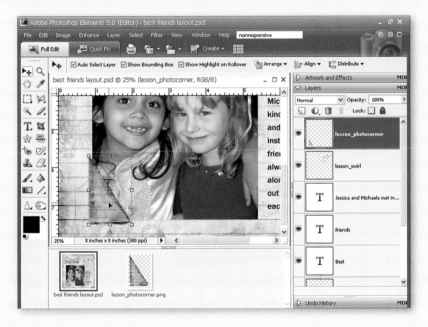

Step 4

Add a photo corner. Choose **File menu> Open> CD>Lesson>lesson_photo corner**; click Open. Repeat steps 1-3.

Quick Guide: Adding Accents

- Open the embellishment file (**File menu>Open> EMBELLISHMENT FILE NAME**).

- Drag and drop (or copy and paste) the embellishment onto the canvas.

- To reposition, select the embellishment layer and use the Move tool to reposition as desired.

- To resize, use the Move tool to activate the embellishment layer. Drag the side, top, bottom, or corner handles to resize.

- To rotate, hover the Move tool over a corner and drag the double arrow left or right (hold down the Shift key to rotate in 15-degree increments).

Lesson 5: Finish and Save

By now your layout looks complete, with expertly placed photos, journaling, and accents, but with just a few tweaks, it will be finished with panache. There are easy ways to give your layout lifelike dimension. Drop shadows and bevel effects give individual elements volume and relief from the scrapbook page. Many designer digital accents have drop shadows already added to them, but you'll most likely want to add them to your photos and possibly your text treatments.

When finished with your layout, save several versions. 1) Save the original layout as a Photoshop native format, unflattened file, which will preserve each independent layer for future edits. 2) Save a high-resolution, full-size, flattened file for printing. 3) Save a low-resolution, smaller size flattened file for e-mailing and Web publishing.

To save an unflattened version of your file (so you can still edit the document if you wish), choose **File menu>Save As**, name your file, and choose the PSD format. This stands for "Photoshop Document" and means the file has been saved in its "native format."

Once you have a native file saved, it's time to save a high-resolution file for printing. On p. 50, the act of "merging" layers was discussed. Merging layers is great for reducing the file size and saving memory. When your layout is complete, you will want to merge all of the layers together; this is called "flattening." This makes the file easier to print and share. To flatten, choose **Layers palette>More>Flatten Image**. Then execute a Save As (**File menu>Save As**) and choose your desired file format.

Now, you should have two files—the unflattened, full-size, full-resolution document and the flattened, full-size, full-resolution document. To resize the file to create a smaller, low-resolution file, see the Quick Guide on p. 59.

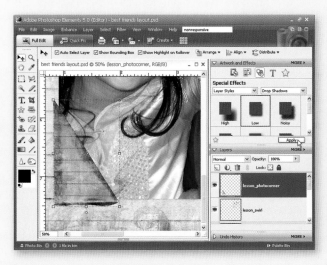

Step 1

To add a drop shadow to text, images, or embellishments, select the appropriate layer. Go to the Artwork and Effects palette in your Palette Bin (if it is not there, choose **Window menu>Artwork and Effects** and the palette will appear on the desktop). Under Special Effects, choose Layer Styles from the drop-down menu. Scroll through the choices and pick a drop shadow (for this lesson, choose Low). Click Apply. A starburst icon will appear next to the layer's name.

Step 2

Customize the shadow by choosing **Layer menu>Layer Style>Style Settings** or double-clicking on the layer's starburst icon. You can change the Lighting Angle, which changes the direction of the shadow, by entering a degree value. You can also adjust the shadow's size, distance, and opacity using the sliders. Click OK to implement your changes. To remove layer effects, choose **Layer menu> Layer Style>Clear Layer Style**. You can also apply drop shadows and other layer effects to text; unlike filters, most layer effects can be applied without having to simplify the layer, leaving them fully editable.

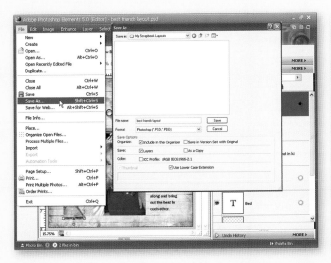

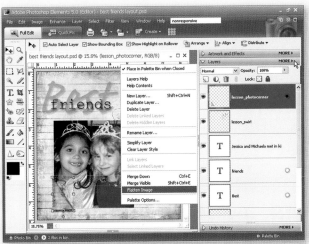

Step 3

Save your layout in native format. Choose **File menu>Save As** and name your layout. The File Format window will say "Photoshop (*PSD *PDD)." This saves your file with all its layers and editing capabilities intact. Choose a location to store your layout and click Save. Your file will now have a .psd extension at the end of its filename.

Step 4

To flatten your image choose **Layers palette>More>Flatten Image**. This merges all the layers into one Background layer. Once you do this, you will no longer be able to edit this document in its layered format. Flattening reduces the file size and also enables you to save it in a format you can print, e-mail, upload to a Web page, or share with friends.

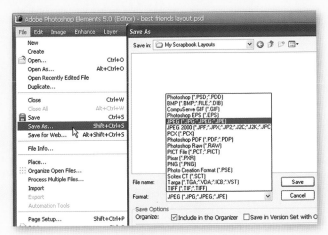

Step 5

Choose **File menu>Save As**. Select the desired file format and rename your file. In Photoshop Elements, you can have two files with the same filename only if they are saved in different formats and therefore have a different file extension, for example "best friends layout.psd" (Photoshop file) and "best friends layout.jpg" (jpeg file). Choose a location to store your layout. Click Save.

Quick Guide: Resizing and Saving

- Select the canvas and choose **Image menu> Resize>Image Size**.

- Inside the dialog box, set the Width and Height boxes for inches. Enter the new desired dimensions.

- To maintain the proportions as you resize, check the Constrain Proportions box. If you are scaling an image with type, make sure the Scale Styles box is checked or the type will not be scaled proportionately to the image. Check the Resample box to keep the resolution the same (select Bicubic when reducing a file size and Bicubic Smoother to enlarge a file size).

- If you are enlarging a file, (for example, if you are enlarging an 8" x 8" layout to 12" x 12") enter 12" into the Width and Height fields, select Bicubic Smoother as your Resampling option, and be sure the resolution is 300 dpi.

- Choose Save As to create a new file with new dimensions while keeping the original full-size file.

- If you are saving a file for the Web, select Bicubic as your Resampling option, and set the resolution to 72 dpi.

Digital Design Basics
Understanding the components of a well-designed page

Once you've mastered the technical aspects of digital scrapbooking, you'll want to focus your attention on the basics of page design. A strong scrapbook page relies upon terrific photos, good use of color, refined line quality, rhythm, balance, and unity. You'll read more about all those factors in the pages that follow.

Pick the Best Photos

The more photos you take, the more likely you are to end up with a handful of truly amazing images. When choosing photos for a scrapbook page, whittle down your images and select only your favorites. Holding on to less-than-great photos will only add to your clutter. Delete them or throw them away.

Find the Focal Photo

One of your selected scrapbook-worthy pictures is sure to be "focal photo" material. It's the photo that yells, "Hey! Look at ME!" Showcase your focal image by enlarging it, giving it a bright, color-popping mat, or applying spot color. Position other page elements so that they point to it.

Find the Photo Within the Photo

Most photos benefit from some cropping. By removing distracting backgrounds, you call focus to your photo subject. Digital photo manipulation allows you to experiment with a variety of potential crops without fear of destroying the original photo.

Choosing the right photo is tough. This artist circumvented the challenge by selecting a photo with sleepy eye contact as the focal image for this page and placing the other images inside a digital filmstrip accent.

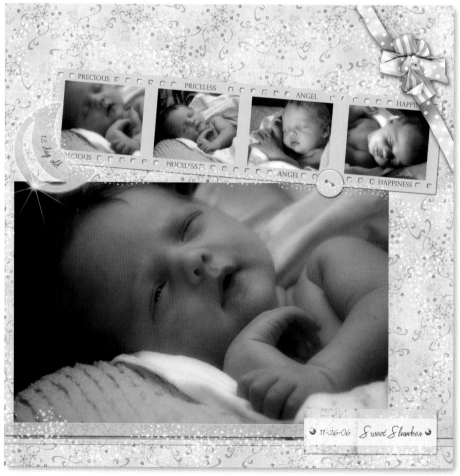

Heidi Knight

two

It's about learning to do that high pitched squeal when she doesn't get what she wants.

And learning to blow kisses when she's getting into trouble.

It's about taking off running when Mommy says "naptime".

And refusing to let anyone else hold her spoon at meals.

It's about telling me when it's time for a story and when she wants "sit me".

It's about spontaneous hugs and kisses and "I ya you"'s.

It's about being Meg at two.

Angelina Schwarz

On this energetic background, a vertical title and digital arrow accent draw the eye to the photograph. Digital stitches line the photo, helping to separate it from the background.

Composing a Photo With Mood

Digital cameras make it easy to experiment. As the photographer, it is your responsibility to enliven your photos by interacting with your photo subjects. Here are some tips:

- Make your subjects move. Ask everyone to jump up and down while you snap away. Put on music to get them dancing. Have them link arms and walk with wide steps.

- Offer artistic direction to your subject. Cue your photo subjects by asking them to pull a face or giving them a feeling to act out (sad, lonely, scared, excited, bummed out, etc.).

- Interact with the subject(s) of your photos. Evoke reactions by making your own silly faces, dancing around, singing loudly, or asking provocative questions.

- Surprise your subject with a new angle. Grab a ladder or a chair to get higher for interesting photo angles. Sink to your belly for worm's-eye views. Photograph from behind the action. Fake 'em out by snapping photos from hip height or capturing the in-between moments.

Use Color With Emotion

Color is your strongest ally in creating exciting pages. When picking colors for your page, look first to the photos. While it is often unwise to select a dominant color from the photo to be the primary color for your layout's palette, you may use it as an accent. Use a color wheel to help select complementary shades for your palette. If your heart is set on using a color combination that fights with the colors within your photos, convert your images to black-and-white. Then you are free to scrapbook with shades that convey the emotion behind your page. Throughout history, certain colors have been linked with feelings and events. Use those associations to your benefit:

- **Red:** Use to show love, anger, power, action, excitement, danger, intensity, attitude, passion, femininity, drama, heat, speed, emphasis, maturity, holiness, wrath.
- **Orange:** Use to evoke earthiness, tropics, sunny days and dispositions, tanginess, lionheartedness, strength, honor, generosity, gluttony, opposition, safety, energy.
- **Yellow:** Use to convey light, cheeriness, hope, cowardliness, prosperity, sensationalism, caution.
- **Green:** Use to conjure thoughts of nature, growth, serenity, fertility, freshness, rejuvenation, youth, money, environmentalism, mobility, balance, luck, liberalism, technology.
- **Blue:** Use to represent clarity, loyalty, discipline, tranquility, scholastics, strategy, sadness, rarities, the universe, work ethic, authority, conservatism, winning, coldness, divinity.
- **Purple:** Use to show royalty, opulence, distinction, psychedelics, the heavens, pretension, bravery, mourning, forgiveness, pride, the unconventional and unexpected.

The bold primary colors in these photos drive home the title of the layout. They are skillfully contained by an earth-tone background.

Lucrecer Braxton

Fall colors shine with intensity in this layout. The Hue/Saturation levels (**Enhance menu>Adjust Color>Adjust Hue/Saturation**) were manipulated to increase the warm tones in the image.

Wendy Tapscott

Using a Color Wheel

Let the color wheel help you discover exciting color palettes.

- **Monochromatic:** Translated, monochromatic means "one color." Monochromatic color schemes are the easiest to master because they rely on different shades, tones, and tints of one color.

- **Analogous:** These color schemes are composed of neighboring colors on the color wheel. The result is a smooth blend of colors for pages that call for color schemes to act as a serene, harmonious backdrop. Example: Red + Red Orange

- **Complementary:** If you need color to create a statement, opt for a complementary scheme. Complementary colors rest directly across from each other on the color wheel and provide maximum contrast. It's best to choose one color as the dominant color and the second as the accent color. These combinations are high energy. Example: Red + Green

- **Split-complementary:** This threesome of color also offers high contrast but with a bit more spice and a bit less tension. A split-complementary scheme is comprised of one color plus the two colors adjacent to its complement (it forms a "y" on the color wheel). Example: Red + Blue Green + Yellow Green

- **Diad:** Because this color scheme is comprised of colors that are neither too close nor too far apart on the color wheel, the result is often a pleasant surprise. Pick a dominant color and then choose a color that is two colors away; you can pick the color on either side of the dominant color. Example: Red + Violet

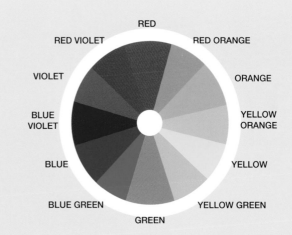

- **Triad:** Three is the magic number for this color combination. Triad schemes are not too bold nor too quiet. They can carry rich and exotic page themes with a sense of grace. To form them, choose three colors that are equidistant from each other on the color wheel. Example: Red Orange + Yellow Green + Blue Violet

- **Tetrad:** For those pages that require a more complex and exciting color combination, tetrad combos can provide that necessary dose of variety. The four colors that make up this scheme hark from two complementary pairs. For best results, pick a dominant color and use the rest as accents. Example: Blue Green + Yellow Green + Red Orange + Red Violet

Layout Design Magic

Once photos and colors have been selected, you are ready to design your scrapbook page. As a novice, look to artists whose work you admire for design inspiration. Re-create the ideas, adding your own unique vision. As you practice designing successful layouts, you'll begin to develop your own layout style and sense of design.

Line Quality

Line quality refers to the appearance of the lines in your layout (the patterns, the style of the fonts, the outlines of design elements such as borders, the edges of accents, etc.). Good designs employ thoughtful use of line quality.

When determining your page's line quality, take your cue from your photos. Are the lines in the images straight and strong or straight and delicate? Do they zigzag with rough edges? Are they soft waves? Mimic these qualities in the design via your choice of patterns and page elements.

Rhythm

A rhythmic design has repeating elements that cause the eye to dance across the page. With a little creativity, any type of page element can be repeated, but the easiest items to repeat are page accents (think about a page that includes a flower border on flower patterned paper). Color can also be repeated, shouting out from unexpected corners, humming along photo mats and frolicking inside doodles.

Elizabeth Tamanaha, Photo: George Lee

Waving lines of text, zigzagging digital rickrack, and a line of polka dots connect the images and elements in this layout that speaks to individual style. The line qualities are varied and contrasting to play up the subject's unique sensibility. The cable-knit sweater was the main source of inspiration for the waves and curves found inside the lines and chosen font (P22 Cezánne).

In one of our last days in Knysna, my mom came up with the great idea to have a picnic at Brenton on Sea, at the Gazebo where we got married. We grabbed some chips, cheese and wine and headed out. It was a beautiful sunset and I got some great pictures. We even got to see a whale quite close to the shore...

Several repeating elements add to the design rhythm of this page. From the bottom up, a row of diamonds from a digital harlequin print border helps carry the eye across a row of detail photos. Monochromatic polka dots spiral, one after the other, inside a delicate print on digital patterned paper.

Mary-Ann Buchanan, Photo: James Buchanan

Scraplifting Etiquette

Scraplifting happens when you "borrow" the creative ideas of others for your own scrapbook pages. Follow these guidelines for using the ideas of others with integrity.

- Give credit where credit is due. If you post your page to an online gallery always credit your source of inspiration.

- When competing, use only your own creative juice. If you are trying to get pages published or win contests, your work should be 100 percent original.

- Don't go overboard. Some ideas have become so popular that they require no attribution. If an idea is everywhere, it's a verifiable trend and needs no attribution.

- Scraplift all you want if you have no intention to publicly share your work.

- Become a better designer. As you scraplift, make note of why you like certain techniques and ideas. As you advance in your art, challenge yourself to build upon these things to develop your own style.

Balance

Balance can be one of the trickiest design skills to master. When conceptualizing a layout, artists must choose between symmetrical or asymmetrical balance. Symmetrical balance means, when split either horizontally or vertically, both sides of the layout are identical. Asymmetrical balance finds equilibrium within a design that can't be halved into identical parts. Balance depends upon visual weight. Thicker, darker, larger elements carry more weight than their thinner, lighter, smaller counterparts. When arranging items on a page, note the weight of each. Once completed, squint at your design. Oddly enough, this helps you determine if visual weight is evenly dispersed, if it pools in corners, or if half of the design weighs more heavily than the other side.

It is easy to build a precise digital layout because most software programs have customized rulers and grids to help you perfectly place elements. Interactive tick marks on the rulers move as you move your tools and your elements. Both rulers and grids are controlled in the View menu. You can change the zero point of the rulers by placing the pointer over the zero-point axis in the top-left corner of the document and dragging to the new, desired location (to reset, double-click the axis in the top-left corner). When you show the grids, they will overlay your layout and help you evaluate the balance of your design.

Unity

Unity is the most abstract of the design principles and arguably the most important. It refers to the "big picture" aspect of your design—does everything work well together; does everything flow? Do the line quality, color, texture, and pattern support the mood reflected in the photos, title, and journaling? Is the layout balanced? Are there unifying, rhythmic elements to tie the page together as an integrated whole?

Rulers and grids provide a visual guide on which to build a balanced scrapbook page. To toggle these on and off, choose **View menu>Rulers** and **View menu >Grids**. In the View menu, you can also choose **Snap To>Grids** and items placed on the canvas will line up with the grid. Customize grid spacing by choosing **Edit menu>Preferences>Grid**.

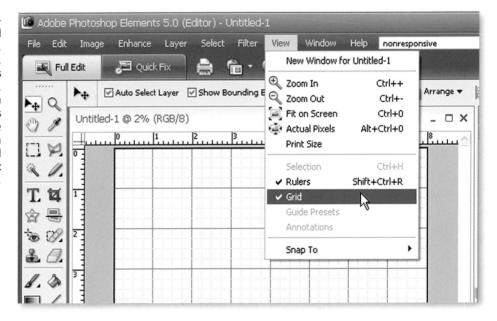

To change the zero point on the ruler, select the Move tool from the Toolbox and position it over the zero-point axis (the square just above and left of the zero points). Drag the guide to the desired place on the ruler (for this example, the guides are at the half-inch mark). Reset the zero point by double-clicking on the zero-point axis.

Although this page is not created with identical halves, if you split this page down the vertical center, the visual weight is equal on both sides. This is an example of symmetrical balance.

Sandra Stanton

Everything about this layout works together to convey a soft, contemplative mood. The soulful look in the little girl's eyes is the inspiration. A soft blue paper with a lightly distressed pattern creates the foundation on which a Victorian tree motif, blue flourishes, and script font (Jane Austen) rest. The photo was enhanced with a distressed digital frame.

Sheila Doherty

Troubleshoot Technical Problems
Understanding and solving computer glitches

When you and your computer are on good terms, work flows smoothly. But suffer a freeze or a hard-drive meltdown and relations quickly deteriorate. There are some steps you can take to keep these frustrations to a minimum, and others that can get you back in working mode fairly quickly.

Geek Speak

A few sentences filled with unfamiliar technical jargon are enough to make anyone mentally check out. Knowing what these terms mean will enable you to better communicate with tech help if your computer ever does suffer some trouble or to even figure out the problem yourself.

Crash

A crash is the mechanical breakdown of a computer. Most use the term generically to describe the state of a nonresponsive computer. A crash happens when the mechanism that reads the data crashes into the mechanism that stores the data. Rebooting is not recommended in a computer crash (you will hear a grinding or squealing sound or all applications will suddenly freeze and require individual Force Quits). Turn off the computer and call tech support.

Data Recovery

After a computer crash, this is the act of trying to retrieve data from the hard drive. Data recovery has become a niche industry in the IT world, so it's readily available, but it comes with a hefty price tag and no guarantee that your information will be recovered. Some applications, such as Adobe InDesign® come with built-in data recovery.

Disk Utilities

For Mac users, this function should be performed monthly as regular computer maintenance. Run this utility regularly to repair hard-disk and start-up issues (**Hard drive>Applications>Utilities>Disk Utilities**). For PC users, a similar tool can be found via the following menu path: **Start>Control Panel>Administrative Tools>Computer Management** and choose Device Manager, Disk Defragmenter, or Disk Management.

Freeze or Frozen

These are terms to describe the state of an unresponsive computer. If a computer is frozen, nothing will move on the screen. The user must reboot. All unsaved changes will be lost. If your computer is frozen because of an unresponsive program, try to quit the program first (see Unresponsive Program) to alleviate this problem. Otherwise, you must reboot. If your computer has one, push the restart button (a smaller button near the power button), or push the power button to shut down fully and then push the power button again to restart.

Recovered Files

These are files that have been found by a data recovery program (or application with built-in data recovery) after a hard-drive crash. Sometimes if your computer freezes, the machine will save a "recovered" or "mirror" file of the document in which you were working. Normally these files can be found in the location where the original document was originally saved (i.e., if you were working on a file that you saved to your desktop when your computer crashed, check the desktop).

Save vs. Save As

To "Save" a file means to save changes to the current document. To "Save As" will allow you to keep the original document unchanged while making a copy, which you must rename. DANGER: You must do this; you cannot have two files with the same name unless they have different file format extensions. If you do not change the name, your original file will be replaced with the new one. Save As also gives you the option to change the location and change the file type.

Unresponsive Program

When an application is not responding, the computer screen is frozen, or the mouse won't move, try to override the application and force it to quit by pushing and holding **Ctrl-Alt-Delete** until the Task Manager opens (Mac: choose **Apple>Force Quit**). While unsaved changes will probably be lost, this is better than shutting down your entire machine.

Virus Threats

Viruses are a real threat to technology, and because of the Internet, almost every computer in the world is linked to another. Viruses can damage your computer by deleting files, destroying applications, and harming the hard drive. More benign viruses will simply load your machine with text, graphic, or audio files that can cause your computer to perform erratically and your system to crash. As a digital scrapbooker, you are particularly susceptible to viruses because you are likely sharing images with friends and family—your computers can pass viruses to each other.

A virus is a computer program that copies itself without the permission of the computer user. Many types of viruses exist. An e-mail virus spreads over e-mail and infects a recipient's address book, mailing copies of itself to all of the e-mail addresses. A Macro virus is spread by infecting Microsoft® Word and Excel documents. Worms are software that prey on security flaws inside a computer network to copy and spread itself. Trojan horses are havoc-wreaking programs that pose as something completely innocent, such as a game, utility, or e-mail attachment.

Once opened, they can send e-mails to everyone in your address book or, worse, steal passwords and data.

Mac users are less susceptible to virus infection because all software installation on a Mac is password protected. PCs are much more at risk, but there are precautions you can take to protect your machine from the spread of viruses. First, be smart about the e-mail attachments you open; if you do not know the sender or if the file attachment name looks odd, delete the file. PC users should also install virus-detection software on their machines and periodically scan their machines for Trojan horses. Symantec™ Norton AntiVirus™ is a for-purchase, downloadable software that will detect and remove viruses from your computer. It also will block spyware and worms and prevent the spread of viral e-mail. Symantec Security Check is free scanning software that can be accessed online through www.geeksquad.com. It checks for unauthorized access to your machine and for Trojan horses.

New viruses are a constant problem, and virus software companies work to alleviate new threats long after you purchase your program. For better protection, update your operating system software regularly.

This artist blasted her way through digital murkiness to find her digital design prowess. The result? A creative digital layout that affirms her can-do attitude.

Angelina Schwarz

TECH SUPPORT!!! (Surviving Digital Disasters)

Technology is powerful, but things CAN and DO go wrong. Because of this, it is imperative to back up your data. Jot down a list of crucial items to be backed up on a regular basis. Schedule routine backups once a month and stick to the schedule (we recommend backing up data at monthly bill-paying time).

"Save and save often" should be one of your mantras. In Photoshop Elements, you have the Undo History palette, which allows you to retrace your steps backward and forward and Undo any saved changes (once you close the session, though, that luxury expires). The Undo History palette resides in the Window menu. By default, up to 50 changes will be saved into this palette, but you can increase that number by choosing **Edit menu>Preferences>General** and entering a number up to 100. If you don't want to commit to experimental changes, you can always save a duplicate copy of the file before creatively exploring.

If you're in the market for a new computer, invest in the extended warranty and protection plan. A one-time investment of a couple of hundred dollars can save you thousands in the long run. Professional tech support is priceless. If you have to call tech support for any reason, follow the instructions inside the "Troubleshooting" section of your owner's manual. Be prepared to answer these questions: Does the problem have a pattern? Could it be related to faulty hardware? Have you recently installed applications or added more RAM?

Veronica Ponce

Large files, like the photo on this scrapbook page, can burden a computer's processor. Additional RAM will speed the creation of your scrapbook pages.

Um, Honey?!

Five things to check before freaking out

1. Is everything plugged in? Thankfully, the solution to any problem is often the simplest. It's possible that someone unplugged something and forgot to plug it back in.

2. Are you running out of memory? The most common reason for a sluggish computer is lack of memory. Investing in more RAM is a good idea.

3. Is your computer the victim of spyware? Spyware programs are third-party applications that attach themselves to computers, without permission, through Internet use. The programs track Internet habits, such as sites visited and products bought, sending the info back to marketing firms. Symptoms of spyware include a crawling Internet connection and lots of pop-up ads. Programs such as Webroot Spy Sweeper can be installed to clean your system and prevent new spyware from leeching onto your computer. Mac users don't have to worry about this because applications cannot be installed onto their machines without their express permission. PC users, go to www.microsoft.com and download free spyware protection. Check this site periodically for new free software. If you have high-speed Internet access, turn on Automatic Update to keep your operating system up to date.

4. Have you been installing software updates? The software on your computer is updated frequently. Inside your Control Panel or System Preferences you can set your computer so that it checks for updates on a regular basis (we recommend weekly). These software updates will help your machine run more smoothly.

5. Have you tried to reboot? If you suspect that your computer is frozen, wait a full minute or two. If it's still not responding, the computer or the application in which you were working is frozen. Try quitting the application first; choose **Ctrl-Alt-Delete** (Mac: **Apple menu>Force Quit**). If the computer is unresponsive, you will need to reboot. Unfortunately, either way, all unsaved changes will be lost.

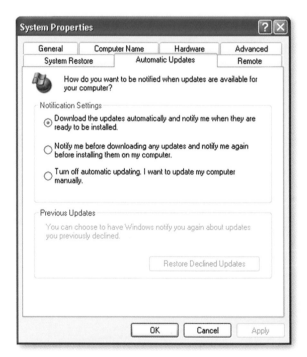

Automatic updates of your computer's operating system are crucial to keep it operating at peak performance. Both PCs and Macs have built-in software that checks for updates when your computer is online.

DIGITAL DIVAS KNOW

Keep this information organized and handy:

- Receipts for everything (equipment, software, servicing, Internet installation, etc.) as well as warranty info
- Type of Internet connection (modem, DSL, wireless, or Ethernet) and corresponding passwords
- Internet service provider and telephone number
- Software registration numbers (you need these to purchase or download upgrades)
- Software installation disks (great idea to keep these together on a blank-CD spindle or dedicated CD storage book as backups; if you purchased downloadable software, burn a copy to disk for a backup)
- Owner's manuals for all computer and computer-related equipment (computer, printer, scanner, camera, software, wireless router, etc.)

wrinkles be GONE!

Shhhh

{I've had a little work done}

blur that mess!

no more deep lines

april 2006

just say NO to LINT

As I was "fixing" this photo, it occurs to me that maybe I get a little carried away. When WAS the last time I just left a photo of myself alone? I'm not a vain person. I don't worry about my appearance when I'm just out and about, but give me a photo, and I CAN NOT leave it alone! Seriously, it's an illness!

I need an INTERVENTION!

Angelina Schwarz

Working With Photos

Pixels are the digital building blocks of visual information, and every digital photo is comprised of them. Your image-editing software allows you to alter a digital photo, pixel by pixel. This chapter provides you with the information you need to perform an assortment of manipulation tricks.

The ease with which you can make digital image adjustments will surprise you. Basic manipulation skills allow you to crop photos, enhance image composition, and rotate images for a clearer perspective. You can also adjust the color, correct lens distortion, and sharpen soft-focus images.

As you grow your digital image-editing skills, you'll discover the power of Selection tools, come to understand the editing flexibility that layers offer, and marvel at the way images can easily be merged, elements removed, and photos transformed.

The longer you spend with your software, the more comfortable you'll be when exploring ways to alter your images. Begin the fun by turning the page to discover handy techniques you'll use again and again.

Image-Editing Basics
Correcting photo flaws and manipulating your images

Your first and most practical adventure in digitally editing your images will be basic photo correction. These corrections allow you to select a specific portion of your photo for correction or manipulation, remove unwanted portions of your photo, correct distortion, rotate an image within the frame, and flip a photo on a vertical or horizontal axis.

Isolating an Element

Selection tools help you isolate elements within a photo for editing. A selection border surrounds the area to be edited (you can edit inside of the border, but the area outside the border will not be affected). The edges of a selected area can be refined with Feathering (softens the selection border) and Anti-aliasing (smooths the edges of the selection). Each Selection tool allows you to corral a portion of your image in a different way. The Mode drop-down menu allows you to adjust the size/proportions of a selection border. Adjusting the Fixed Aspect Ratio controls the width-to-height ratio of the border.

Study the following examples to familiarize yourself with the tools.

Rectangular Marquee: square or rectangular selections

Elliptical Marquee: round or elliptical selections

Magnetic Lasso: complex selections (best for objects with irregular edges/high-contrast background)

Lasso: precise freehand selections

Polygonal Lasso: complex rectangle or square selections

Magic Wand: selections by color.

Magic Selection Brush: intuitive selections by color and contrast—click and/or drag the tool across the area and a red mask will appear. Don't select too large of an area; the small red circular mask (achieved with just one click) resulted in a selection identical to the photo on the left.

DIGITAL DIVAS KNOW

Different tools have different strengths. Most scrapbookers use only one or two selection tools for the majority of tasks. However the smart scrapbooker evaluates the task and then selects the best tool.

Expert Tips: Selection Tools

Use the following suggestions for more precise selections:

- Zoom in to fine tune your selection.

- Adjust Tolerance. "Magic" Selection tools select pixels within a similar color range. To increase or decrease the sensitivity of these tools, adjust the Tolerance. Low values select more similar colors and higher values select a broader color range.

- With the Magic Selection Brush, use the Foreground brush (with the plus sign) to add to a selection. The Background brush (with the minus sign) will remove areas from a selection.

- While the Polygonal Lasso tool was created for straight-edged objects, you can lay down as many segments as you need for precise selections of any shaped object. Use the Delete key to immediately remove an ill-placed segment.

- The Polygonal and Magnetic Lassos require you to draw entirely around the perimeter of the object, closing the loop on the exact point where you started. These tools have shortcuts to help you close the loop without being exactly on the point (this is useful if you have a lot of points and can't tell where you started). If you want to close the loop with a freehand magnetic segment, double click or press Enter and the tool will close for you. To close the border with a straight segment, hold down the Alt key and double click.

Adjusting a Selection

Once you have made a selection, you might need to add to or subtract from it, make more than one selection, or select the intersection of two selections. Rather than start over, you can adjust the selection.

To Add to a Selection

Activate your selection and either

- choose your desired Selection tool and click the Add to Selection icon in the Options bar, or
- choose your desired Selection tool and hold the Shift key. A plus sign will appear next to the tool icon to signal the addition, and you can make a new selection. If you wish to expand the original selection, click and drag, overlapping the existing selection. If you simply want to create an additional separate selection, click and drag outside of the existing selection.

To Subtract From a Selection

Activate the selection and either

- choose your desired Selection tool and click the Subtract From Selection icon in the Options bar or
- choose your desired Selection tool and hold the Alt key. A minus sign will appear next to the tool icon to signal the subtraction. Drag the mouse over the area you wish to subtract.

To Intersect Two Selections

To select the intersection (areas that overlap) of two selections, make the first selection with any of the Marquee or Lasso tools. Keep the selection active and either

- choose the Intersect With Selection icon on the Options bar and hold the Shift key while you drag the tool to overlap the previous selection; when you release the tool, the new selection will include only the areas where the two selections overlapped, or
- choose your desired Selection tool, hold down Alt and Shift keys while you click and drag a new selection that overlaps with the original; when you release the tool, the new selection will encompass the areas of both selections.

Magic Extractor

Hiding under the Image menu is an amazing knockout tool called the Magic Extractor. It makes selecting oddly shaped and complex forms easy (see the step-by-step on p. 77).

All Selection tools, except the Magic Selection Brush, have four choices in the options bar: (from left to right) New Selection, Add to Selection, Subtract From Selection and Intersect With Selection.

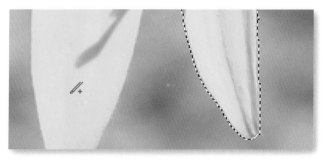

Some areas were missed with the first use of the Magic Selection Brush. Choose the Add to Selection icon (found in the Options bar), and click on areas to add. For Selection tools that do not have this in the Options bar, press the Shift key and a plus sign will appear next to the tool.

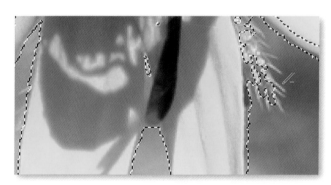

In this use of the Magic Selection Brush, too much information was selected. Choose the Subtract From Selection icon in the Options bar and click on the area you wish to deselect. For Selection tools that do not have this in the Options bar, press the Alt key and a minus sign will appear next to that tool.

With Selection tools, you can create multiple separate selections, create a selection that combines all of your selections or only select the areas that overlap (called an Intersection of Two Selections).

Step 2

Use the Magic Marker-style tool with the plus sign to place red dots on the foreground items you wish to keep. Strategically place dots in areas of highlights, shadows, and color variance to better define it. Use the Magic Marker with the minus sign to place blue dots in the background, using the same principles for light, shadow, and color variance. Handy zoom and hand tools are built in to help you see the file you're working on. Click Preview to see the selected area.

Step 1

Open the Magic Extractor by choosing **Image menu>Magic Extractor.** It has a dialog box that opens with its own tools and options.

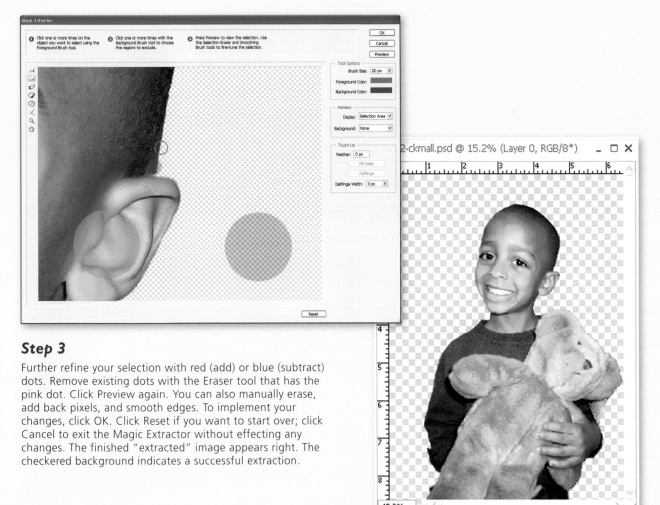

Step 3

Further refine your selection with red (add) or blue (subtract) dots. Remove existing dots with the Eraser tool that has the pink dot. Click Preview again. You can also manually erase, add back pixels, and smooth edges. To implement your changes, click OK. Click Reset if you want to start over; click Cancel to exit the Magic Extractor without effecting any changes. The finished "extracted" image appears right. The checkered background indicates a successful extraction.

Cropping an Image

Images are cropped to improve their composition by removing unnecessary information and bringing attention to the focal point. When cropping images of people, you want to avoid cropping at a person's joints; otherwise they tend to look amputated. Crop instead at the chest, biceps, waist, mid-thigh, or mid-shin. For landscape shots, resist the urge to place the horizon line in the middle of the image; instead, fill the image with two-thirds sky or two-thirds land, whichever is more interesting. You can also crop photos into panoramics or thematic shapes.

To crop images, select the Crop tool. You can only use this tool to crop images that are opened independently, not on images that already have been placed onto a canvas. Otherwise, you will crop the entire canvas. To crop a photo on a layer, use the Rectangular Marquee (see right).

To crop your photo, choose the Crop tool from the Toolbox. Drag it across your photo; the selection will have a bounding box that you can resize or rotate. When satisfied, click on the green checkmark to confirm.

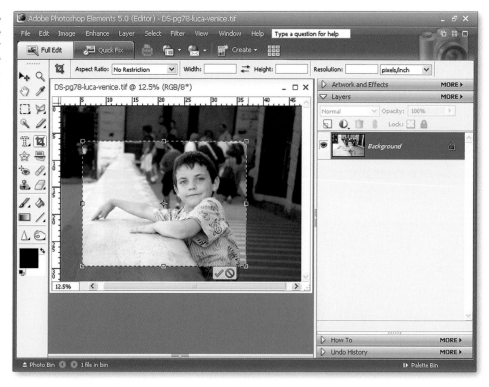

The original photo (above) has a distracting background. The subject becomes the focus once the photo (right) is cropped.

Original

If your camera does not have a panorama setting, you can easily create one from any size photo by selecting and deleting the top and/or bottom.

To trim a photo on a layer or scrapbook layout, use the Rectangular Marquee to make a selection across the width of the photo. Choose **Select menu>Inverse** and push Delete. By using the Rectangular Marquee tool and not the Crop tool, the canvas will remain intact.

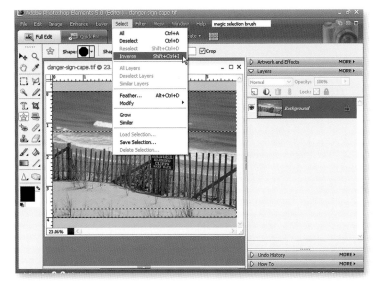

The Cookie Cutter tool (the star-shaped tool in the Toolbox) will crop photos into shapes. Choose it and then choose a shape from the drop-down menu (shown above) in the Options bar. Click and drag the shape over the image until the image fits inside the shape as desired. When you release the tool, the portion of the image outside the shape will disappear and a bounding box will flank the crop. Adjust or move the box and click on the green checkmark to confirm.

Transforming an Image

Unless creating an abstract image, a photographer's goal is to capture an image that accurately represents an object's shape, size, and form. That's tough even for a professional to achieve. Distortion is the culprit when photographed images look skewed or bowed. This often occurs when you use a wide-angle lens on your camera. To correct simple distortion, look in the Image menu for Transform, which offers three ways to correct distortion: Skew, Distort, and Perspective. These functions work in similar ways, and this illustration focuses on Skew. To appreciate the subtle differences between the three, experiment with your own photos. For complex distortion problems, opt for the Correct Camera Distortion filter.

Skew is an easy solution to simple image distortion. It works especially well with architecture. In the original photo (left), the building and the tower appear to be leaning. In the corrected photo (above), the structure has been straightened giving it a more natural appearance.

Step 1

Open your image file and turn on the Rulers and Grids (**View menu>Rulers and View menu>Grids**). Then choose **Image menu>Transform>Skew**.

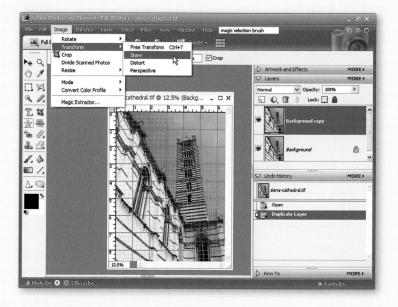

Step 2

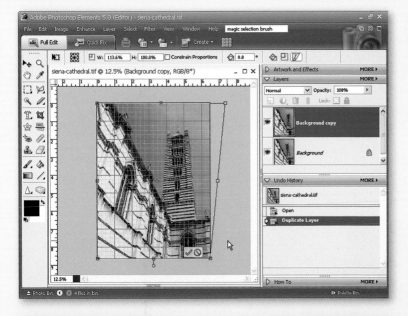

Drag the corners until the tilted image in the photograph is square to the grid. Click the green checkmark to confirm the change. Crop the resulting image to eliminate any unwanted areas.

Variation: Step 1

You can correct distortion both vertically and horizontally at the same time with a special filter. Choose **Filter menu>Correct Camera Distortion**.

Variation: Step 2

In the open dialog box pull sliders and experiment with the angle until you are satisfied with the results. Click OK. Crop the resulting image to eliminate unwanted areas revealed by the image correction.

Rotating an Image

Most often photos are imported into a computer from a digital camera in a horizontal format. This means that photos shot vertically must be rotated to be viewed correctly. Images photographed at odd angles also may need to be rotated. Images that are crooked due to the photographer inadvertently tilting the camera while snapping the picture can also be straightened with rotation.

You can rotate in 90-degree increments, right or left, and 180 degrees by selecting **Image menu>Rotate** in the options menu. You also can rotate by choosing Custom, which is also found in the Image menu. If you choose the custom option, a dialog box will pop up asking you to enter a numeric value for the rotation. Or, you can use the Move tool to rotate a photo. Click on the photo with the Move tool and a bounding box with squares on the corners and sides will appear. Hover the Move tool over a corner and a curved, double-arrow will appear; drag left or right to rotate. Hold down the Shift key while dragging to rotate in 15-degree increments.

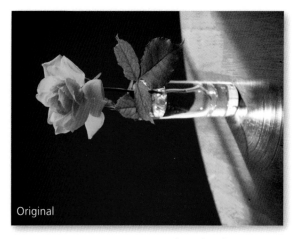

Rotating images is simple and makes viewing photos in a folder or the Photoshop Elements Organizer much easier.

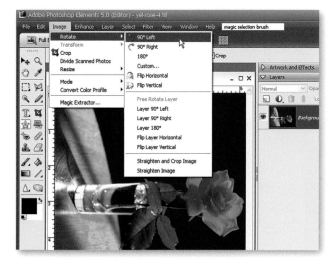

To rotate images and scrapbook canvases, you can choose any of the following from the **Image menu>Rotate** drop-down menu: 1) selection 90 degrees left, 2) selection 90 degrees right, or 3) selection 180 degrees, or 4) Custom. To rotate on a layer, choose options from the **Image menu>Rotate Layer** drop-down menu.

You also can rotate images on a layer using the Move tool. Hover the Move tool over a corner and drag the double-arrow right or left to rotate. Hold down the Shift key to rotate in 15-degree increments. Click the green checkmark to confirm.

Flipping an Image

Sometimes an image must execute an "about face," meaning it will benefit from being flipped to reflect its mirror image. The need for this maneuver becomes obvious as you enter the design stage of your layout. Most often an image is flipped because, in its original form, the placement of the photo on the scrapbook page makes it appear as if the photo subject's eyes are looking off the layout instead of toward its center. This directs the eyes of anyone looking at the layout off the page as well. To flip your photo, choose **Image menu>Rotate** and you will find options to flip the entire canvas or items on a layer.

You can flip a selected item, a layer, or your entire canvas. To flip a photo, choose **Image menu>Rotate>Flip Horizontal** or **Flip Vertical**. This will flip the entire canvas, not just the selected image. To flip a layer, choose **Image menu>Rotate>Flip Layer Horizontal** or **Flip Layer Vertical**.

Shannon Taylor

When the artist sketched the design for this layout, it became obvious that the support photo in the lower right corner needed to be flipped. Otherwise, it would have directed the reader's eyes off the page.

Color and Exposure Adjustment
Compensating for less-than-perfect light

Photographers spend countless hours learning how to adjust camera settings so that the final image accurately reflects the photo subject. It can be difficult to accomplish, and that's why image-editing software offers a variety of options for color and exposure correction.

Determine Your Workflow

Begin by making sure that you are working in the RGB color mode. For the most effective color adjustment, crop and resize the photo before adjusting the color. View the image at 100 percent, then check the Preview box in any dialog box to view color changes as you apply them. You may click the Reset button or Cancel if you are not satisfied with the results. What follows on the next five pages is the recommended sequence of adjustments for

expert color correction. If you prefer easier options, use the Quick Fix mode for one-touch remedies (see p. 85 for a list of choices).

1. Correct the Skin Tone

In a photo of a person, the subject's skin tones are used as a benchmark to guide color correction. Look at the skin tone. Does it have a color cast—in other words, does it look red or, worse yet, green? If the skin tone is perfect, move on to Enhance the Exposure on p. 86. If not, proceed to **Enhance menu>Adjust Color>Adjust Color for Skin Tone** in Photoshop Elements. This will bring you to a dialog box that allows you to adjust for a number of factors (see the image right), including tan and blush. When a pleasing skin tone is achieved, click OK.

Images with poor skin tone can appear faded, yellowed, and even garish. For the best scrapbook layouts, take the time to make your photo subjects look their best.

A little bit of an age difference.
A little mutual admiration.
Same independent spirit.
Marco & Ellie became good
buddies on our trip to Cape Cod.
After a sunny morning on the
beach they both loved to have
lunch at our favorite clam shack.
Watching them both grow is a joy.

Sheila Doherty

Original

Poor skin tone (above) was easily corrected (right) with the Adjust Color for Skin Tone function; note that the color for the entire photo is adjusted as well as the skin.

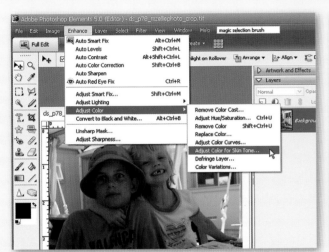
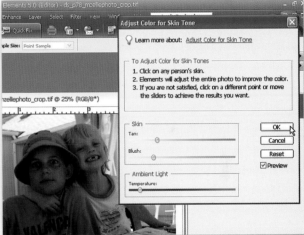

Step 1

Open your image file and choose **Enhance menu>Adjust Color>Adjust Color for Skin Tone.**

Step 2

A dialog box and the Eyedropper tool will appear. Click on a portion of the image with the tone you want. Photoshop Elements will then adjust color for the entire image based upon that tone. To refine, drag the Skin sliders to adjust the amount of tan and blush. Use the Temperature slider to make the colors warmer or cooler; click OK to implement changes.

Quick Fix: Color Adjustments

When adjusting the color of an image in the Quick Fix mode, opt for only one of the Auto Correct commands (inside the Enhance menu). If your first choice does not give the desired result, click Reset and try another. The commands are as follows:

- **Auto Smart Fix:** To effect overall color balance and improve shadow/highlight detail

- **Auto Levels:** To heighten contrast and eliminate color cast
- **Auto Contrast:** To adjust overall contrast when there is no discernible color cast
- **Auto Color Correction:** The most powerful command; to correct shadows, highlights, and midtones, and to remedy contrast and color cast

2. Enhance the Exposure

An image that has been perfectly exposed will show full tonal range. Tonal correction is the adjustment of the light and dark areas of your image. When making tonal corrections, you adjust the shadows, highlights, midtones, brightness, and contrast of an image. Under the **Enhance menu>Adjust Lighting** menu, you will discover three ways to affect the tonal range of your image.

- **Levels:** A histogram becomes visible in the dialog box. Use the sliders on the histogram to adjust the shadow, highlight, and midtone values. This is your most powerful exposure tool.
- **Shadows/Highlights:** Adjustment of these will affect the full tonal range; Levels adjusts the values of shadows, highlights, and midtones, but Shadows/Highlights affects the amount of detail.

 Inside this dialog box, you can move the sliders to brighten dark areas (shadows) of your image or darken bright areas (highlights) as well as increase or decrease the amount of contrast within the midtones.

- **Brightness/Contrast:** Because it affects an image's overall brightness and contrast, this is a great tool to use for a quick universal tonal correction.

3. Fix Hot Spots and Deep Shadows

If you need to make acute adjustments to areas of shadow and highlight, use the Dodge and Burn tools, which are located in the Toolbox, under the Sponge tool. These tools are great when you want to make localized exposure changes without affecting the rest of the photo.

 Use the Dodge tool to target areas of the image that are underexposed (too dark) and the Burn tool for areas of the image that are overexposed (too light). Select either tool in the Toolbox and drag it over the area that needs correcting. The Dodge tool will lighten the area, and the Burn tool will darken the area. Adjust the degree of change in the Options bar. The Range option determines whether you want to affect shadows, highlights, or midtones.

Slight underexposure makes this photo dark. Correcting lighting levels improves the quality of the image across the entire photo (right). You can use a Selection tool to select specific areas and adjustments will only apply to the selections.

Step 1

Begin by going to the Layers palette; choose Duplicate Layer from the More drop-down menu, rename if desired and click OK. To enhance exposure, choose **Enhance menu>Adjust Lighting**. Levels, Brightness/Contrast, and Shadows/Highlights are all located in this menu.

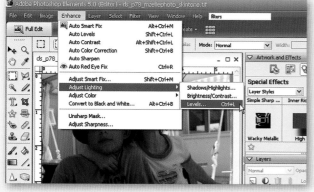

Step 2

Adjust Levels in the dialog box by entering values or adjusting the sliders. The graph inside the histogram represents the number of pixels in the image and therefore is a measurement of the image detail in regard to shadows (dark areas), highlights (light areas), and midtones (middle gray areas).

 This histogram shows full tonal range, meaning the darkest areas of the image are black and the lightest are white. Notice how the bars extend all the way to the edges of the graph. If the bars stop short of the edges, the darkest and lightest pixels are a varying shade of gray. If the bars favor the left or right sides of the histogram, the image is characteristically shadowed or highlighted.

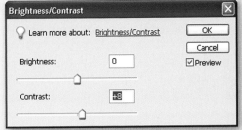

Step 3

In the Brightness/Contrast dialog box, move the sliders to achieve your desired results.

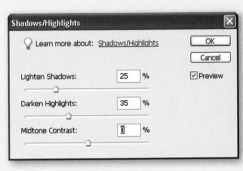

Step 4

In the Shadows/Highlights dialog box, move the sliders as desired.

The shadows in the photo on the far left are too dark. The Dodge tool was dragged over the shadow areas to lighten them and even the tone of the image. Customize this tool in the Options bar (above).

Although improved with the Dodge tool, the photo (far left) has several hot spots (too much light). This is evident in the highlight on the hair, nose and cheek. The Burn tool was dragged over these areas to darken them and bring out lost detail (left). Customize the Burn tool in the Options bar (above). The Exposure option will give you the most control for both the Dodge and Burn tools. To affect an area gradually, enter a low value and repeatedly drag the tool over the area that needs correcting.

4. Adjust the Color Balance

Most scanners and digital cameras have a slight color bias. To correct the bias, you must adjust the color balance by increasing or decreasing the amounts of red, green, and blue in your image. When you make adjustments to one color, you are in effect adjusting the spectrum of color by changing the mix of color in the image.

When the colors are balanced, tones will reproduce accurately. This is most evident in neutral grey and white areas of the photograph.

The Hue/Saturation menu offers the most flexibility in adjusting the color balance. It features three sliders to give you control over the following: 1) hue, or color, of the image; 2) saturation, or the intensity of the color; and 3) lightness, or the tints and tones found within the resulting color spectrum. Think of these in regard to ink: Hue is the color of the ink; saturation is how much ink; and lightness is how much white or black you want to add to the ink to lighten or darken the color, respectively.

The building and shutters are too green and the flowers are flat in the photo above; simple adjustments in Hue/Saturation balanced the photo to accurately reflect the building's true colors.

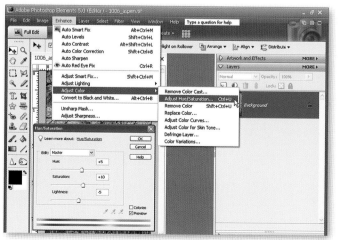

From the Enhance menu choose **Adjust Color> Adjust Hue/Saturation**. Move the sliders as desired and click OK.

You can use Hue/Saturation to convert an RGB grayscale photo to a sepia print. Choose **Enhance menu>Adjust Color>Adjust Hue/Saturation**. Click the Colorize box and drag the Hue slider left. Adjust the Saturation as desired. To convert a color photo to RGB grayscale, see p. 93. In the Artwork and Effects palette there are also sepia effects: **Photo Effects>Image Effects>Tint Sepia** or **Layer Styles>Photographic Effects>Sepia**.

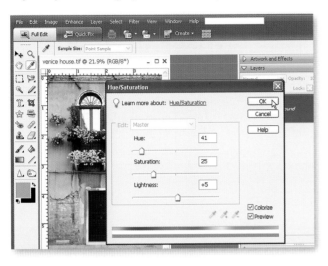

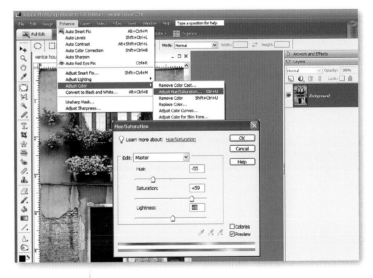

For color that sizzles, adjust the Saturation slider to the right. Likewise, you can adjust the Saturation slider left to mute the colors.

DIGITAL DIVAS KNOW

In digital scrapbooking, you can change the color of anything—images, text, and elements. When you purchase or download digital page elements (papers, accents, overlays, brushes, etc.), you can alter their colors to suit your needs. Just as you would adjust the Hue/Saturation for a photo, you can adjust it for individual accents. Don't alter an original file; duplicate and rename it first!

More Color Adjustment Tricks

Learning the workflow model described on the previous pages will, with practice, result in expert color and exposure adjustment to any image. What follows are more great tips for working with color.

Easy color cast correction

If your image has a color cast, you will notice a shift in overall color toward red, green, blue, or yellow. The cast could be the result of a monitor, scanner, and/or printer in need of calibrating. If you are working with a scan of a traditional print, it could be the photo lab's fault. If it's an image from your digital camera, the cast may stem from the lighting in the photo. It's a good idea to calibrate your monitor (see p. 34) before you begin making color cast corrections.

There are two methods to correct a color cast: additive and subtractive approaches. With the additive approach, you need to increase the complement to the color cast. For example, if your image has a red cast, increase the amount of green. If it has a blue cast, increase the amount of orange. With the subtractive approach, you decrease the amount of the color evident in the cast.

In Photoshop Elements, the default color mode is RGB, which means you must increase or decrease red, green, or blue to make color adjustments. You can make these adjustments across the entire photo or just to midtones, shadows, or highlights. Use the Color Variations function in the Enhance menu to make quick changes; for more precise changes, choose **Enhance menu>Adjust Color>Adjust Hue/Saturation** and change individual colors (under the Master drop-down menu). You can also choose **Enhance menu>Adjust Lighting>Levels** and change individual colors (under the RGB drop-down menu).

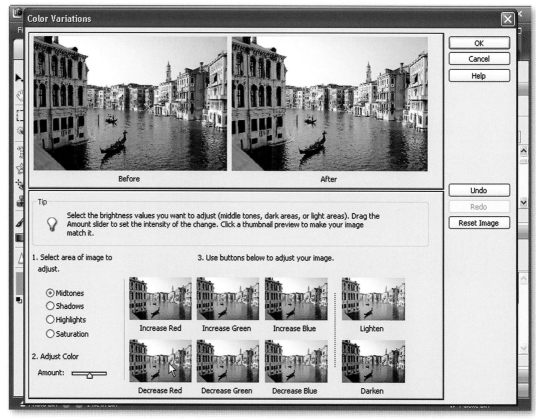

The Color Variations function is a great place to learn about the effects of red, green, and blue on a photo and make quick adjustments. In the Enhance menu, choose **Adjust Color>Color Variations**. When the dialog box appears, Photoshop Elements will provide a series of thumbnails of your image from which you can increase or decrease red, green, or blue. Further refine the color changes by adjusting the sliders for either the Shadows, Midtones, Highlights, or Saturation.

The photo above has a red cast. With Remove Color Cast, the photo was corrected in one easy step. See the dialog box below for more information.

An easy way to correct color cast is to choose **Enhance menu>Adjust Color>Remove Color Cast**. Click on an area in your image that accurately represents true white, black, or neutral gray, and the command will correct the overall color based on the selection.

Paint With Light

If you use light to your advantage, you will take better photos and spend less time digitally correcting them.

- **Know your ISO:** ISO is the speed of film. Film speed is determined by how much light is needed to capture an image. Most digital cameras have an ISO setting that you can adjust in accordance with individual lighting situations. Fast film (800 ISO and higher) needs less light and is perfect for low-light situations or high action. Medium-speed film (400 ISO) is all-purpose; it works well outdoors if the light is not too bright nor too dark. Slow film (100 - 200 ISO) needs more light, so use this setting in bright-light situations or where maximum color saturation is desired.

- **Know that light changes:** Light changes hour to hour and season to season. In most cases, you will find the most flattering light at dawn and dusk. Mid-day light is strong and casts harsh shadows. In the spring and summer, the light will be warm and glowing. Fall offers great light, but as the temperature of the air cools, so does the temperature of light. Light in the colder months is harsher, casting hard shadows, and has a cooler (bluer) tint.

Change the Color

Upon occasion you'll want to change a single color in your photo. Maybe it clashes with other page elements. Or maybe you want to alter the color to make an object visually pop (for example, a person wearing a blue shirt in front of a blue background). You can select and replace a color either across the board or inside of a selection of the image. Under the Enhance Menu, choose **Adjust Color>Replace Color**. When the dialog box opens, you will see sliders that allow you to adjust Hue, Saturation, and Lightness. The Fuzziness slider can be dragged to blend the edges of the new color into the background.

This grey wagon (left) was easily changed to green (right) using the Replace Color function.

Step 1

To change the color inside a portion of an image, choose **Enhance menu>Adjust Color>Replace Color**. A dialog box will open; move your pointer outside the box and onto the image. Click on the color you wish to replace. The selection will appear white in the image preview of the dialog box. Under Replacement options, move the sliders for Hue, Saturation, and Lightness to achieve the desired replacement color; Hue affects the color, Saturation affects the color's intensity, and Lightness affects the color's brightness (adding white or black).

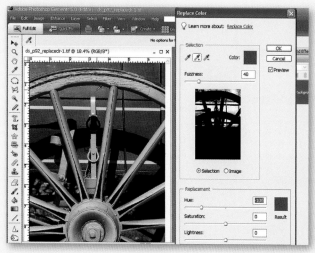

Step 2

If you want to add to the selection, choose the Eyedropper with the plus sign and click on the image to select areas to apply the replacement color. To remove from the selection, choose the Eyedropper with the minus sign and click in the image to deselect areas.

Step 3

Use the Fuzziness slider to blend the new color with surrounding areas. You can also use the slider to expand (drag right) and contract (drag left) the color selection.

Converting to Black and White

Converting an image to black and white can be a purely artistic decision, but it can also be very practical. You can have a photo with great composition but nasty colors. Or you might have a wonderful close-up with a distracting background. Both problems can be solved by converting the image to black and white. There are three ways to accomplish this: 1) choose **Image menu>Mode>Grayscale** (you will not be able to colorize the photo with this option, since it is no longer in RGB mode); 2) choose **Enhance menu>Adjust Color>Remove Color**; and 3) choose **Enhance menu>Convert to Black and White** (Elements 5.0).

Original

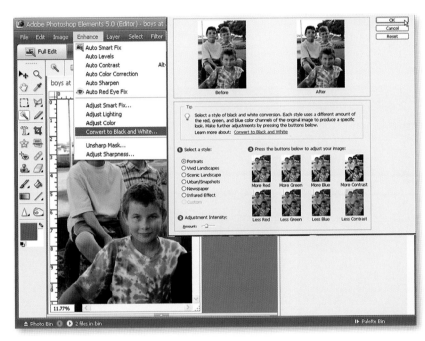

The colorful clothing, flowers, and a flagpole were distracting (top left photo). Converting to black and white brought attention back to the subjects (top right). Under the Enhance menu, choose Convert to Black and White. A dialog box (left) will appear with a preview image. Inside the dialog box are preset options for different effects.

Adjustment Layers

As you advance in the realm of digital scrapbooking, you'll begin exploring the advantages of working in Adjustment Layers.

- **What are Adjustment Layers?** Adjustment Layers are a great way to execute precise color and tonal adjustments on an image without altering the pixels of the original. They exist as a layer over the Background layer.

- **What are the benefits of Adjustment Layers?** If you are making several adjustments to an image, you run the risk of losing image quality. Stacking several Adjustment Layers allows you to make many changes without losing image quality. You can also change your mind and have the unaltered photo available in your layout.

- **How do you create an Adjustment Layer?** Activate the topmost layer that you want to affect. If you only want the Adjustment Layer to affect a portion of the layer, select that portion. Then, do one of the following:

1. If you want the Adjustment Layer to affect all of the layers below, click the Create Adjustment Layer button (it looks like a circle with half of it shaded) at the top of the Layers palette. Choose the type of adjustment you want in the pop-up menu.

2. If you want the Adjustment Layer to affect only one layer, choose **Layer>New Adjustment Layer> ADJUSTMENT TYPE**; press Ctrl-G (Mac: Cmd-G) or choose **Layer menu>Group with Previous Layer.**

Photo Retouching
Repairing damage and eliminating imperfections

Once all color and exposure concerns have been corrected, it is time to polish your pictures by fine-tuning composition problems; repairing tears, water damage, scratches, or dust particles; eliminating red-eye; and removing blemishes. Tonal adjustments made during color correction may sometimes reduce detail, but sharpening (**Enhance menu>Adjust Sharpness**) will help restore it.

Clone Stamp Tool

Get familiar with this tool because it is great for duplicating small details as well as correcting images. It copies, or samples, pixels from one part of your image to replace over another. You'll use it to repair tears, dust, scratches, holes, or to duplicate an object from your image to hide an unsightly element. The clone stamp is ideal for duplicating both solid and finely textured surfaces.

The Clone Stamp tool can be customized in the Options bar. Change your brush type, size, and opacity for greater control. The more you customize the brush to match the size and shape of the item or area you are sampling, the cleaner the results.

Original

The Clone Stamp tool was used to duplicate the football in the photo above. The cloned football was then placed in the image numerous times (right).

The clone stamp is also ideal for hiding distracting items. In the photo above, a portion of the grass was cloned and used to cover the bright orange football that appeared in the original photo (far left).

💡 DIGITAL DIVAS KNOW

When working with the Clone Stamp tool, if you select Align from the Options bar, the sample area will follow the stamp no matter how many times you start and stop dragging. If you deselect this option, the stamp will revert back to the original starting point in the sample area. Deselect this option if you want to repeatedly copy a specific item to different locations.

Choose the Clone Stamp tool from the Toolbox; customize it as desired in the Options bar. Hold down the Alt key and click on the area you wish to sample. Move the Clone Stamp tool to the target area you wish to correct; click and drag the Clone Stamp tool until you are satisfied.

Original

Save damaged heritage photos (above) by scanning them and then repairing dust, scratches, and even tears with the Clone Stamp tool (left).

Healing Brushes

Healing brushes work very much like the Clone Stamp tool, however they have intuitive blending capabilities. They are best used for removing skin blemishes, dark circles, and other distractions, such as slight differences in tonality in specific areas of an image. Customize the brushes in the Options bar to suit your needs.

- **Healing Brush:** This tool copies pixels from a portion of your photo to repair an area with similar tonal and textural quality. The wonder of the Healing Brush is that it blends together the copied area with the background to which it is being applied.

- **Spot Healing Brush:** When it comes to small details, such as specks and facial blemishes, you'll find that this tool offers a one-click fix. Select the tool, customize the brush, and click on the imperfection.

Original

The photo above has significant flash glare on both faces. The Healing Brush was used to correct the problem by copying pixels from skin without glare (right).

Photo: Jaime Vanecko

Select the Healing Brush tool, adjust the brush size in the Options bar (above), and hold down the Alt key. Click on the sample area (skin without glare). Then click and drag the tool over the target area (skin with glare, right).

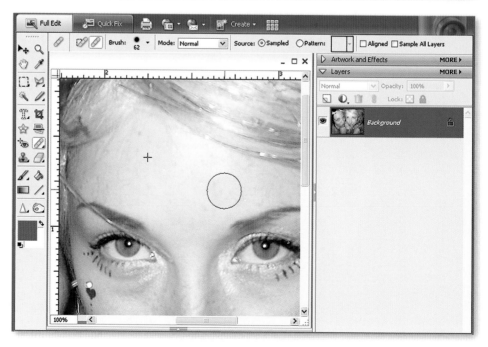

Original

Blemishes are a thing of the past with the Spot Healing Brush tool. Select a brush size just slightly larger than the blemish. Then zoom in, click on a blemish, and watch it disappear.

  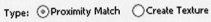

Size: 13 px ▶   Type: ● Proximity Match   ○ Create Texture   ☐ Sample All Layers

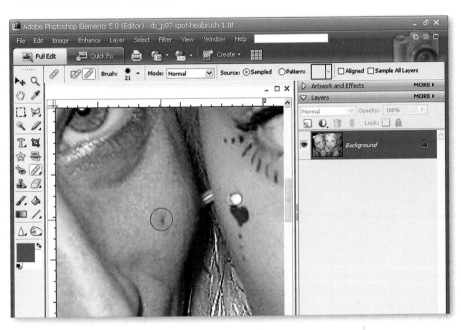

Use the Options bar to customize the Healing Brushes. For the Spot Healing Brush, you can choose between Proximity Match and Create Texture in the Type category. Proximity Match allows the brush to sample pixels around the edge of the brush that will be used to make the repair. Create Texture samples the pixels directly below the brush to create soft texture. When using the Healing Brush, you can choose between several blending modes. Normal is the default and usually works best, but experiment for desired results.

DIGITAL DIVAS KNOW

Photo retouching can be as easy as applying a photo-fixing filter. "Noise" is the digital equivalent of graininess in printed images. This can be reduced with filters. Choose **Filter menu>Noise** and you will have a choice of Add Noise, Despeckle, Dust/Scratches, Median, and Reduce Noise. Experiment until you achieve the desired results.

Image-Manipulation Tricks
Altering photos for impact

Image-editing programs offer artists a tremendous number of options for manipulating photos. In fact, there is very little that you CAN'T do to your image. We've narrowed down a selection of techniques that are not only cool and popular, but also practical enough to be useful for your scrapbook layouts.

Create a Ghost Background

This technique is great for layouts that employ a photo as a background image. It scales back the opacity of the photo so that other elements, such as text, can be layered on top. If you like the look of vellum on traditional scrapbook pages, you can use this technique to create a vellum overlay effect on a digital layout. You can also use this technique to create frames, titles, and journaling blocks (see bottom right). Follow the steps on the right for a custom ghost effect. You can also choose an existing effect (you can't select the color or the level of opacity), select the image layer, and choose **Artwork and Effects palette>Layer Styles>Visibility>Ghosted.**

Ghosting a photo (above) is a great way to create a custom background for your layout (right) that complements but doesn't compete with the main photo.

Rocky Mountain Fall

September brought heavy snows, so this early October warm spell was a gift. The Aspens were in full color, the snow mostly gone and the temperature in the high 60s. A perfect fall day for a hike.

Shannon Taylor, Photo: Andrea Zocchi

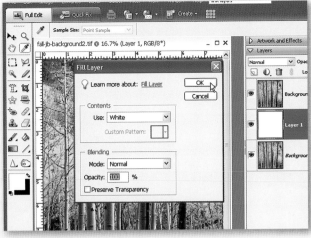

Step 1

Open a photo and select the Background layer. In the Layers palette, choose **More>Duplicate Layer**. Name the new layer and click OK.

Step 2

Create a new layer and fill with white (**Edit menu>Fill Layer>White>OK**). Reposition the white layer below the duplicate layer.

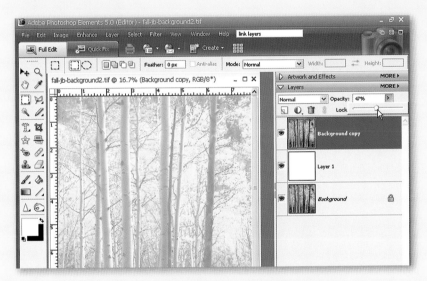

Step 3

Select the duplicate layer. In the Layers palette, click on the right arrow of the Opacity window and a slider will appear. Move the slider to the desired degree of transparency. Choose **File menu>Save As** and rename if you are working on an original photo file.

Variation

Follow steps for ghosting, then select the ghosted layer and the white layer. Click the Link Layers icon on the Layers palette. On the ghosted layer, use the Rectangular Marquee tool to create a square or rectangle in the middle. Choose **Select menu>Inverse** and delete the outside frame of the ghosted image (the same area of the white layer will also be deleted). The photo will now have a ghosted area in the middle.

Spot Color

Spot color is one of the most popular digital image-manipulation techniques. Photographers use it in their gallery prints. Print media uses it on magazine covers, in advertisements, and in article photographs. Scrapbookers use it on all types of layouts, tinting the cheeks of subjects in scanned heirloom photos and colorizing flowers held in a child's hands in a black-and-white picture.

What a cute little "bathing beauty" you are. I have been giving you baths in my sink each morning and you love to look in the mirror at yourself + at me. You are starting to outgrow the bathroom sink - you have to cock your head to the side to lay down. I am amazed each and every day at how much you have grown + changed. I can't wait to see your little personality start to emerge as you grow and mature.

❦ ♡, Mom

Heidi Knight

Nothing distracts from this breathtaking image of a baby cozied up in a bath towel. Soft spot color was used to allow the blue of the towel to cradle the baby girl's adorable face.

Step 1

Open the photo and convert to black-and-white (see p. 101 for instructions). Use a Selection tool to select the item to which you'd like to add color (see pp. 74 - 77 for instructions on isolating an element).

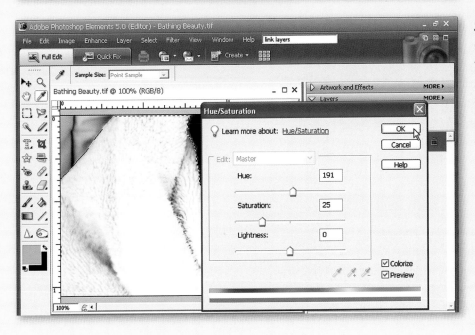

Step 2

Choose **Enhance menu> Adjust Color>Adjust Hue/ Saturation.** Check the Colorize box and drag the Hue slider to find the desired color. Click OK and Deselect (**Select menu>Deselect**).

DIGITAL DIVAS KNOW

Before dedicating time to fixing or manipulating a photo, it is important to determine whether the image is worth the effort. Great images show emotion, context, excellent composition, and interesting perspective. Technicalities such as poor lighting, a slight blur, or an odd color cast can be fixed; emotionless images cannot.

Filters and Special Effects

In the digital realm, the terms "filters" and "special effects" refer to digital commands that alter images in interesting and sometimes fantastic ways.

Filters let you change the look of your images. They can be applied to a photo, a selection, or an entire layer. They are found under the Filter menu. It's a good idea to apply filters to a duplicated layer, which allows you to re-edit the photo at a later date without having to backtrack. Also, you may have to adjust the photo before or after you apply the filter to get the desired effect. Try applying the same filter twice for enhanced results. To try a variety of filters with a preview and customizable options, choose **Filter menu>Filter Gallery**. If you want to apply filters to Text, Fill, or Shape layers, they must be simplified first

(duplicate the layers prior to this to maintain the original).

The Artwork and Effects palette also contains filters as well as additional options for creating unusual looks with your photos, such as overlaying them with a blizzard or a brick pattern (if this palette is not in your Palette Bin, choose **Window menu>Artwork and Effects**; Mac users choose **Window menu>Styles and Effects**). The Artwork and Effects palette is also the place to find three-dimensional effects such as bevels, drop shadows, and metal/plastic effects. Double-click on a filter or effect in the palette. A preview of your image will appear along with a dialog box that provides options for controlling the intensity of the selected filter or effect. Click OK to accept the filter or effect or Cancel to reset the image. Further customize the effect by choosing **Layer menu>Layer Effects>Style Settings**.

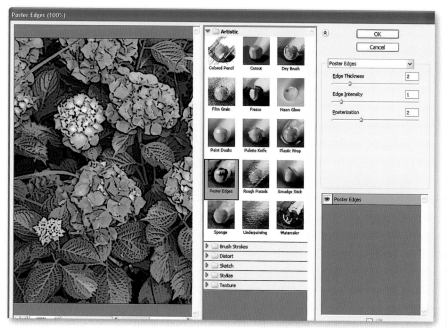

Under the Filter menu, you can select individual filters from drop-down menus under the various categories. For one-stop shopping that allows you to experiment with filters in a preview mode, choose **Filter menu>Filter Gallery,** and a dialog box (above) will appear; click on a filter and you will see how it would look applied to your image. Inside the Artwork and Effects palette (right) you will find backgrounds, filters, photo mats, and other one-touch decorative elements. The drop-down menu on the top left of the palette offers Effects, Filters, and Layer Styles. The drop-down menu on the right lists the corresponding options for the Effects, Filters, and Layer Styles, respectively.

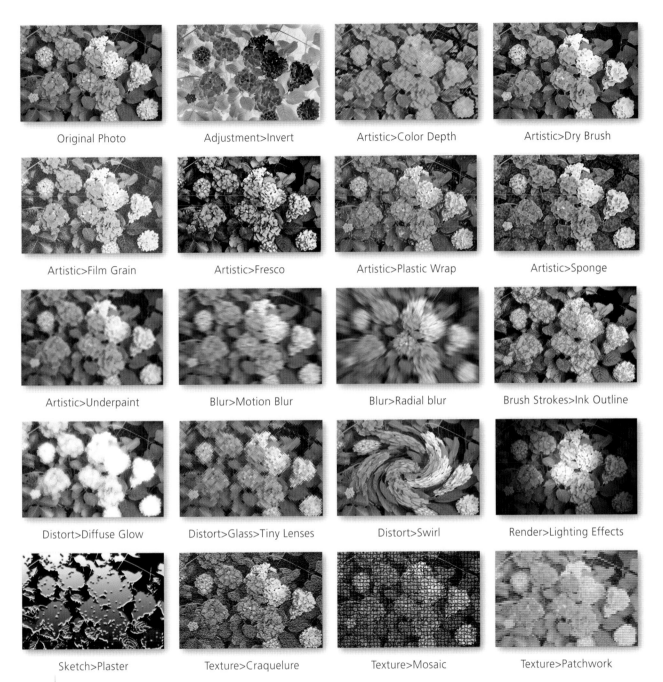

Original Photo

Adjustment>Invert

Artistic>Color Depth

Artistic>Dry Brush

Artistic>Film Grain

Artistic>Fresco

Artistic>Plastic Wrap

Artistic>Sponge

Artistic>Underpaint

Blur>Motion Blur

Blur>Radial blur

Brush Strokes>Ink Outline

Distort>Diffuse Glow

Distort>Glass>Tiny Lenses

Distort>Swirl

Render>Lighting Effects

Sketch>Plaster

Texture>Craquelure

Texture>Mosaic

Texture>Patchwork

DIGITAL DIVAS KNOW

If you can't find the filter or effect you are looking for, chances are you can download it. Plug-ins are special-effect and filter files that can be downloaded and installed into your image-editing software. Many are free. Begin your search at www.adobe.com/prod-ucts/plugins/photoshop. When installed, the new plug-ins will appear at the bottom of the Filter menu.

The filter gallery above shows how filters mimic an artist's toolbox, with effects that transform photographic images into chalk renderings, charcoal etchings, watercolor paintings, and more. You can apply several filters to one photo. In the Filter Gallery dialog box, the icon at the bottom right will allow you to add a New Effects Layer on which you can add another filter effect.

Photo Effects With Brush Tools

Brush tools are your ticket to some of the coolest and easiest effects in digital scrapbooking. Brushes are responsible for distressed edges on photos and background papers, funky textures, and even digital rubber stamping. Most image-editing software programs have hundreds of brushes from which you can choose. Photoshop Elements allows you to create your own from scratch or to customize existing brushes.

Your basic Brush tool has hundreds of styles in built-in brush libraries. They can be found by clicking the drop-down menu just left of brush size in the Options bar; this menu offers a visual preview of the brush styles. But don't forget that a lot of other tools have brush-like tips, such as the Eraser, Blur, Sharpen, and Clone Stamp tools.

All of your Brush tools can be optimized in the Options bar. Experiment with the widths of each, which can range from 1 pixel in diameter to as large as 2500 pixels in diameter. You can change this width while you are working with your Brush tool by pressing the] key to increase or the [key to decrease the diameter. You can also adjust the blending and opacity modes to the desired effect. The Airbrush icon in the Options bar will slow the paint flow and intensify the color density as you create with your brush. If you have a graphics tablet, adjust the Tablet Options in the Options bar to affect your tablet's pen pressure.

Click the More Options button (paintbrush icon) on the Options bar to find a Brush Options palette. This palette gives you ultimate control over any new brushes you create as well as existing ones. All of the options relate to the brush stroke. You can control the following:

- **Spacing**: How much space is there between strokes? The higher the value, the more space between.
- **Fade**: How long of a stroke does your brush have before it runs out of paint, so to speak?
- **Hue jitter**: What color is your paint? Jitter determines the rate at which the color switches from foreground to background. The values of saturation also fluctuate.
- **Hardness**: How defined are the edges of your brush stroke? A high percentage is more solid than a lower percentage.
- **Scatter**: How far apart are your bristles spread? High percentages will spread a brush tip.
- **Angle**: What angle will the brush tip be? Think of this in terms of a calligraphy pen with skinny or wide nibs.
- **Roundness**: What is the shape of your tip? The value you enter will determine the range between a perfect point or mashed and squished bristles.

Custom Brushes

Custom brushes are easy to create, especially when you use existing brushes as a foundation. You can modify any of the brushes in the Brushes library or you can download custom brush sets that other artists have created and modify them. In fact, the CD at the back of this book contains a brush set with which you can experiment.

Step 1

Select the Brush tool. Click the Brush Styles drop-down menu on the Options bar (above) and select a brush to customize (right).

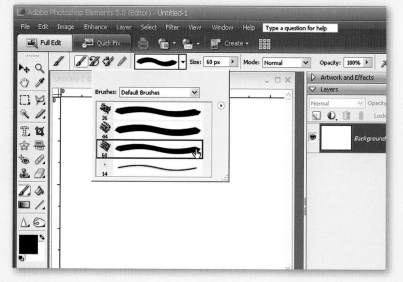

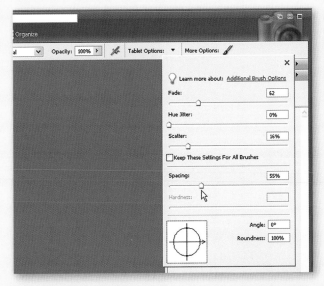

Step 2

Click the More Options button to open the Brush Options palette (left). Adjust the sliders to modify the brush properties and adjust the Angle and Roundness, if desired. When satisfied, click anywhere on the Options bar to close the palette. Adjust the Size slider if desired. Custom brush shown above.

Step 3

Reopen the Brush Styles drop-down menu and click on the right arrow to reveal another drop-down menu; choose Save Brush. Type a name into the dialog box and click OK. The custom brush will appear at the bottom of the list on the Brush Styles drop-down menu.

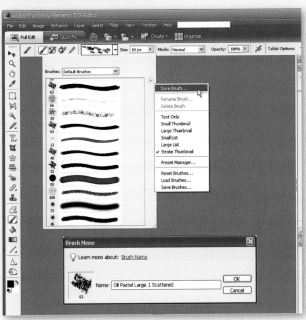

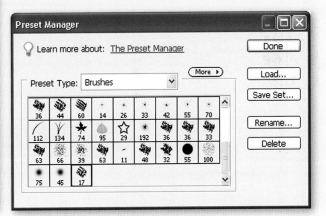

Saving New Brushes

Save custom-created brushes by creating brush sets. When you create a new brush, it exists only temporarily in the Brush Styles drop-down menu. Once you reset the Brush Preset palette or choose a different brush, the new brush is no longer available. If you save new sets of brushes, you won't lose them. You can create sets for your favorite brushes, new or pre-existing, to make them easier to locate.

Create a New Brush Set
• Create a new brush.

• Choose Preset Manager from the Brush Styles drop-down menu.
• Hold down the Ctrl key (Mac: Cmd) and click the brushes you wish to include in the set from the thumbnail view.
• Click Save Set to open the Save dialog box.
• Name your brush set and click Save.
• Quit and relaunch Photoshop Elements and the new set will appear in the More menu on the Preset Manager and the Brush Styles drop-down menu.

Custom Brush From a Photo

You also can create brushes from photos or images of scanned objects. Brushes can be created from botanicals, interesting textures, and more. Think creatively! When creating brushes from photographic objects, keep in mind that the color information will not translate, only the tonal values and shape. You'll want to choose images with high contrast for that reason.

Step 1

Open the image from which you are going to select a shape to use to create a custom brush. Select the object from the image using one of the Selection tools (for more information on Selection tools, see pp. 74 - 77).

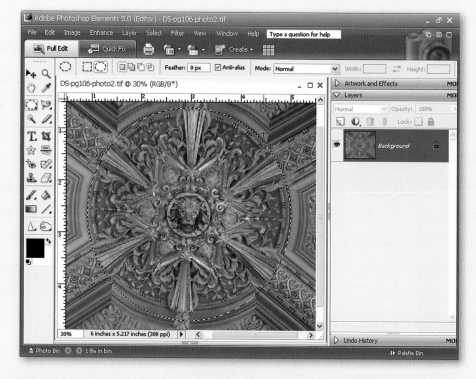

Step 2

Choose **Edit menu>Define Brush from Selection** and a dialog box will appear with your new brush visible inside a Preview box. Name your brush and click OK.

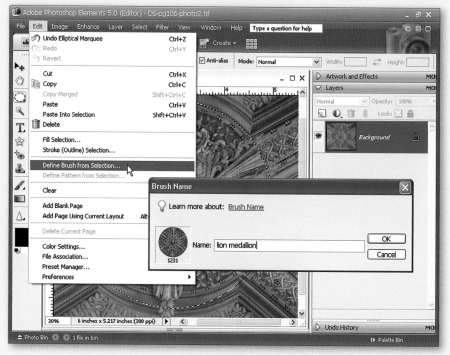

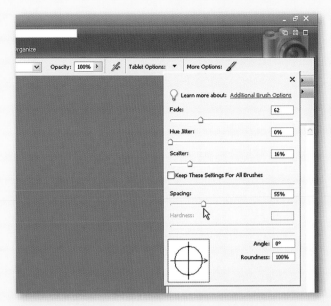

Step 3

Select the new brush and click More Options on the Options bar to open the Brush Dynamics palette (left). Modify the brush as desired. Custom brush shown above.

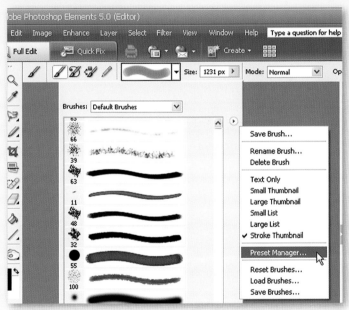

Step 4

Select the Brush tool and open the Brush Styles menu from the Options bar. The new brush will be at the bottom of the Brush Styles menu. Click the right arrow and choose Preset Manager to save new brush in a brush set for future use (see p. 105 for instructions).

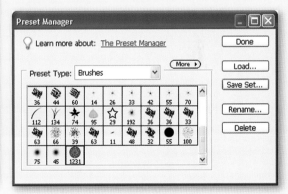

Installing Downloaded Brushes

Downloaded brush sets need to be installed in your image-editing software. Place new brushes in the Brushes Preset folder (**Hard drive>Program Files> Adobe> Photoshop Elements>Presets>Brushes**). Then, to load the brushes, open a photo in Photoshop Elements and choose the brush tool. In the Options bar, open the Brush Presets palette.

There will be a small triangle, click it and another menu will open. Choose Load Brushes. A dialog box will open; choose the brush set from the brush folder. Quit and restart Photoshop Elements and your new brushes should appear in the brush styles drop-down menu.

Photo Composites

A photo composite brings two or more pictures together to create a new work of art. Composites can be sophisticated, surreal, or intoxicatingly funny. You could build a composite to create a family-tree portrait from scanned heirloom photos, compose a wild collage with your favorite images, or drop the picture of a photo subject onto a new background. There are so many ways to meld photos that it is impossible to note even a fraction of them. This is where your imagination comes to play. Let it run wild.

When you create a photo composite, you work with a "target" image and a "source" image. Your target image is the foundation of your composite. The source image will be the image you are merging with either a part of or the entire target image.

It's a good idea to edit the images for color and exposure correction prior to creating the composite. But because the images exist on their respective layers, you can make further adjustments and/or enhancements once they have been combined.

When saving your photo composite, it is especially important to save the file in the native format. That way all of the layers are intact and available for adjustments farther down the line.

The artist assembled this composite panorama then added the photo of the two boys taken earlier in the hike.

Photos: Andrea Zocchi

Step 1

Create a new canvas, the target image, and then open the source images. Copy and paste the images into the target image (**Edit menu>Copy; Edit menu>Paste**).

Step 2

Use the Magic Extractor or Selection tool of your choice to knock out any elements you wish to add to the composite without backgrounds.

Step 3

Copy and paste them to the target image (**Edit menu>Copy; Edit menu>Paste**). Use the Move tool to resize and reposition images.

Step 4

Adjust photos as needed to match each other in tonal and color qualities (**Choose Enhance menu>Adjust Color>Adjust Hue/Saturation** or choose **Enhance menu>Adjust Lighting>Levels**).

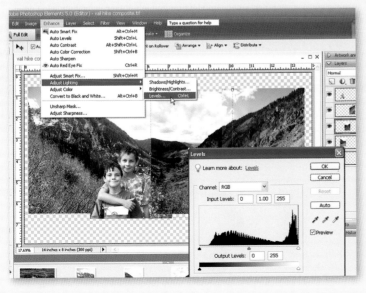

Juicy

berries

scrumptious

RED

Summertime

yummy

Mason Jars

Robby 2006

Shannon Taylor

Letter-Perfect Text

It's time to put to bed notions that successful journaling features alphabet letters marching like regimented soldiers along ruled lines of notebook paper. When you become a digital scrapbooker, you have license to step outside the ranks and blissfully break the rules. You'll find yourself stacking, bending, stretching, squishing, and squashing text to maximize the impact of your layout. And you'll discover (with relief) that since "oops" choices of font, point size, and color can easily be deleted and redone, you are much more likely to extend yourself creatively, taking chances you might not have before. Once you have determined exactly what you want to write on your page, this chapter will make the technical aspect of adding written words to your layout easy!

Digital Lettering Basics
Discovering all the possibilities

Digital scrapbooking is all about convenience, choice, and creative control, which extends from the placement and manipulation of photos to the creation of text. A digital scrapbooker has an enormous number of lettering options available. Fonts are certainly the most versatile and popular lettering tools, but other choices exist as well.

Alphas

A traditional paper-and-glue scrapbooker has letter stickers, chipboard letters, letter die-cuts, etc. A digital scrapbooker has "alphas" (also known as digital letter stamps or letter brushes), which are sets of individual letter files (sets usually contain 26 files but some include both letter cases, numbers, and symbols) digital designers can add to their layouts in the same fashion as an embellishment (see pp. 56 - 57). In appearance, alphas mimic all of the popular paper lettering styles. But unlike the traditional scrapbooker, the digital scrapbooker can reuse her lettering supplies and customize the size, color, pattern, and texture of the letters.

Fonts

A font is a set of letter or symbol characters. A font exists as a single file, which is downloaded and installed onto a computer's hard disk. An enormous variety of fonts are free to download.

Preprinted Digital Accents

The digital equivalents of preprinted transparency overlays, quote stickers, phrase stickers, and even stamped phrases are widely available. These drag-and-drop accents are inexpensive and, like alphas, can be used again and again and customized to suit a digital scrapbooker's needs and preferences.

The most "delightful" part of this title was the ease with which it was created. The word "delightful" is a drag-and-drop digital word-art accent from a kit by digital artist Jen Wilson. The rest of the title was written with Elegant font. Courier New font was used to write the journaling.

Kira you are just such a sweet girl you are so fun to be around and make me laugh often. Your smiles warm my heart and every time I see you I'm glad that I get to be a part of your life. You are a truly delightful little girl.

Peta Stokes

It was April 2005. Micro Soccer season for Ben & Annie, with Kurt coaching Annie's team.

It was cold. Too cold for April. In fact, it snowed that day. And, Meg, patient, as usual, sat quietly in her stroller to watch the game.

I looked down and snapped this photo. Then, I turned my attention to the game. The game where Ben was walking when he should have been running. And, asked to sit out after one quarter. And, we realized something was wrong. We discovered on Monday that he had Mono, but little did we realize what else lay on the road ahead.

And here is our sweet Meg, along for the ride with all of us. resolutely peaceful, patient, and though she never realized it, of course, a very special blessing of hope & joy for each of us.

an extraordinary

an extraordinary day

blessing

Angelina Schwarz

The painterly script lettering that supplements this title is an example of an alpha. Alphas can be purchased on digital scrapbooking Web sites. Once purchased, the Web site will direct you to a link that, when clicked, will start the down-loading process. Most often, the folder of files will be down-loaded onto your desktop. The alphas on this page were part of a digital kit called "A Common Bond" by Valerie Fowler and downloaded from www.thedigichick.com.

DIGITAL DIVAS KNOW

When you import an alpha onto your page, it will appear as a new image layer. That means you can manipulate it just as you would any other image—alter its size or color, apply a filter, and more.

Acquiring and Installing Fonts

Fonts can come from a variety of sources. Most software programs are equipped with a selection of fonts, fonts can be downloaded from the Internet, and they can also be purchased on a CD. Discovering font depositories is as simple as performing an Internet search for the word "font." Narrow the search by including descriptors such as "script," "block," or "graffiti."

Which Fonts Will Work With Your Operating System

Historically, PCs and Macs have not used the same font files, though there is an increasing number of cross-platform fonts being developed. Many times fonts are available for both operating systems, or fonts can be converted from one platform to the other.

Several font formats exist, but the three most common include PostScript (Type I), TrueType (Type II), and Open-Type (Type II). Your computer should be able to handle any of these formats with one exception: Mac users can only use PostScript fonts if they are running OS X or later. Type II fonts are the most user-friendly and will print better on consumer-level printers. They should not require the installation of a font management program, such as MasterJuggler by Alsoft.

When downloading or purchasing a font, be sure that the font is compatible with your operating system. If considering an OpenType font, which is a true cross-platform font, check to see that it is compatible with your image-editing software.

How to Install Fonts

The fonts that were bundled with existing software already running on your computer normally don't require special installation beyond the software installation. Downloaded fonts and fonts on CD do. Many times, these fonts are ready for installation once downloaded or acquired from the CD. Other times, the font files are "compressed" and need to be "expanded." Special programs such as WinZip for PC and StuffIt for Mac and PC can be purchased online and downloaded to perform these functions. Once you install a font, it will be located on your hard drive (**Start>Control Panel>Fonts for PC; Hard Drive>Library>Fonts** for Mac). After installation of a font, all of your word-processing and image-editing software programs should be able to access it.

Fonts that are "zipped" (PC) or "stuffed" (PC/Mac) have been compressed; large files often are compressed to increase the speed and efficiency of downloading or e-mailing. Zip utilities are programs that enable you to "unzip," "unstuff," or "expand" compressed files. Allume Systems StuffIt Expander® is available free for both PC and Mac.

To unzip a compressed file, download and install the StuffIt software onto your computer. Download a compressed file and double-click the compressed file to open StuffIt Expander. Depending upon the software used to compress the file, StuffIt Expander will either unzip it automatically or prompt you through the process. **PC users:** If you are running Windows XP, right-click on the file and an option to "expand" will appear in the drop-down menu. **Mac users:** If StuffIt Expander does not open automatically, drag-and-drop the file onto the utility's program icon. Macs with OS X will place the icon in the dock; otherwise, it can be found in the Applications folder on the hard drive.

LOVE
THESE
TWO

OUR BOND
is unbreakable
you guys are my life
for always xoxoxox me

Laura McKinley

This page uses a distressed typewriter font, a font style incredibly popular with scrapbookers because of its nostalgic feel. Several typewriter fonts can be downloaded from the Internet for free. Their versatile style makes them great for all types of pages.

10 Free Font Web Sites

Thousands of free fonts are available for download. Here are just a few sites to try. To find more sites, type "free fonts" into your Internet search engine.

www.1001freefonts.com
www.1001fonts.com
www.dafont.com
www.simplythebest.net/fonts

www.free-fonts.com
www.fontfreak.com
www.myfonts.com
www.acidfonts.com
www.dingbatdepot.com
www.searchfreefonts.com

Font Management

Organize fonts on your hard drive in clearly marked folders. A font utility program can be purchased for those who collect fonts by the hundreds. Please note that if you are using an older operating system such as Windows 98 or Mac OS 9, you will need to install Adobe Type Manager Light for accurate display of Type 1 fonts.

Screen Fonts vs. Print Fonts

If your digital page designs will never leave your computer, use all the fonts you want! If you wish to print, be aware that some fonts are designed strictly for monitor display. If a font has a geographic location name, such as Monaco, Chicago, or Geneva, chances are it's designed only for screen display. If you do not use a print font, the resulting font will look "jaggy" or pixilated on your printout.

To locate the Fonts folder on Windows XP, go to **Start>Control Panel>Fonts**. Simply drag and drop fonts into the folder.

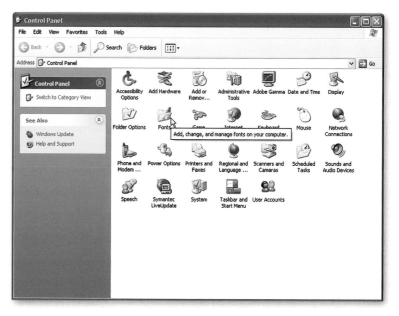

To locate the Fonts folder on a Mac, go to **User Home Folder>Library>Fonts**. You can drag and drop fonts into this folder.

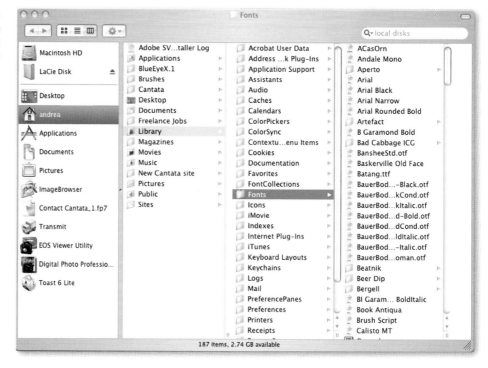

Avoiding Font Problems

As a student of digital scrapbooking, you'll diminish headaches and increase your pleasure in working with your fonts by keeping a few tips in mind.

- **Don't use pirated fonts.** Font-sharing is illegal. You also open yourself up to viruses and unreliable or corrupted fonts. Use what you have and then buy or download free fonts from a reputable manufacturer that offers updates and support for its fonts.
- **Back up your fonts.** Create a master font library and back it up on CD. If you do have a corrupted file, you can simply dump your fonts and reload from the clean master disc. Put your fonts in alphabetical folders to make your search easier.
- **Check your fonts folder for duplicates.** Your program wasn't designed to decide which one to use, so the resulting conflict could lead to error messages, printing problems, or even a freeze.
- **Load the whole font.** Type II (which includes TrueType or OpenType) fonts have only one file, but Type I (also known as PostScript) fonts come in two files for screen resolution and printing information.
- **Don't overload your fonts folder.** This will slow down the operation of your computer. Load the fonts you use all the time and any specialty fonts you've selected for a given project.
- **Use a font-management program.** If your font library is large, or you are overwhelmed by the idea of troubleshooting font problems, consider running a font-management program. These programs load and unload fonts, look for duplicate files, and try to resolve errors from corrupted files and font conflicts. Macs running OS X come loaded with Font Book. Third-party programs are also available. Microsoft has a listing of recommended manufacturers of fonts and font programs on its typography Web site, www.microsoft.com/typography/links; click Type Foundries.

If you use a plethora of fonts on your layouts, as is the case on this layout, good font-management is essential. Consider using a font management application that allows you to create font categories. This will enable you to easily find the perfect font for your scrapbook page.

Wendy Tapscott

Formatting Text
Striving for readability

Once you have a font library in place, you can move to hands-on formatting of text. Creative use of text is an excellent skill to master. Remember that text is as much of a design element as the embellishments on your scrapbook page. As you strive for creativity, however, don't sacrifice readability. Tweaking text can make the experience of reading it more pleasurable. As you lay out the text on your page, keep the following points in mind.

Line Length

If you flip through a stack of magazines and newspapers, you may notice that nine out of 10 times, most of the text is formatted in narrow columns. There is a good reason for this: At normal reading distance, the human eye has trouble focusing on text wider than 3½ inches. All text does not need to exist in columns, but keep the aforementioned point in mind before you stretch text ALLLL the way across a page. You want your reader to follow along comfortably without losing track of her place.

Alignment

Alignment refers to how text sits within its block. Text can be left-justified, centered, right-justified, or justified. The word "justified" in regard to text alignment simply means "flush." Left-justified text is aligned flush with the left margin; right-justified text is flush with the right margin; and justified text is flush with both the right and left sides. Centered text is centered between the page margins.

Typically, left-justified text is the easiest to read, but you may want to opt for right-justified text if the text is abutted on its right side by a photo or other anchoring page element. You may wish to justify text on a layout that is rigidly structured. Centered text can have a poetic quality and is best used with airy text blocks. Long bodies of text should be left-justified.

If the Type tool is selected you can change the justification of text in the Options bar. For this layout, the arrow is pointing to the left justification button; the text reflects this selection. For instructions on adding and formatting text, see pp. 54-55.

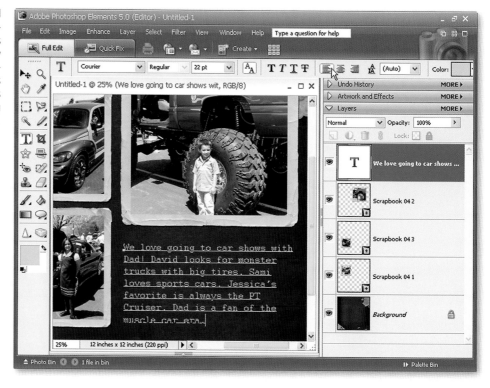

The text on this digital layout is right-justified, which means it is flush with the right margin. This proved a good design decision because the text block rests along the right edge of the page. The lines of text are short and easy to read.

These were some of my favorite moments from our trip to Southern Pines earlier this year. It's a rare occasion that you'll goof around with me like this. And while it took a little begging and pleading on my part at first, eventually you came around. Judging by your smile, I think you wound up having a pretty good time, although you'd sooner eat a bug than admit it. But all is good because I've got proof. So on those days when I have again been relegated to the bottom of the food chain, I will look through these photos, remember how loud we laughed and reassure myself that sometimes you do, in fact, enjoy hanging with me, despite all outward appearances and evidence to the contrary.

Andrea Chamberlain

SPECIAL CHARACTER CHEAT SHEET

		Mac	PC
©	(Copyright)	Option g	Alt 0169
¢	(Cent)	Option 4	Alt 0162
°	(Degree)	Shift Option 8	Alt 0176
÷	(Division)	Option /	Alt 0247
•	(Bullet)	Option 8	Alt 0149
...	(Ellipsis)	Option ;	Alt 0133
—	(Em Dash)	Shift Option -	Alt 0151
–	(En Dash)	Option -	Alt 0150
"	(Inches or Seconds)	Shift '	Shift '

Mac users: If the keystrokes below don't give you quotation marks, check your program preferences.

'	(Quotation marks, single)	Left: Option]	Left: Alt 0145
'	(Quotation marks, single)	Right: Shift Option]	Right: Alt 0146
"	(Quotation marks, double)	Left: Option [	Left: Alt 0147
"	(Quotation marks, double)	Right: Shift Option [	Right: Alt 014

Darn Text Looks...Odd

You've written the right words, chosen the best fonts, conceived the most incredible layout design. Yet when you add your text, something just isn't right. If your text needs a little something and you can't put your finger on it, consider adjusting the tracking, kerning, and/or leading.

Photoshop Elements is a powerful design tool, but beyond basic titles and journaling blocks, its text functions are limited. If you need to make fine adjustments or want to get really creative with text, you may want to consider either a vector-graphics or desktop-publishing application designed specifically to handle text. Adobe Illustrator® (vector-graphics) or Adobe InDesign® (desktop-publishing) are two programs that will allow you to capably manipulate text. Tracking, kerning, and leading can be adjusted in the Options bar of these programs.

Tracking

This term refers to the space between words. Deft tracking will enhance the readability of your text. Adjust the tracking to alleviate unequal spacing inside horizontal lines of text or to remedy over-hyphenation. It's best to apply tracking to an entire body of text instead of a single line.

Kerning

Kerning is the amount of space between each letter within a word. Use it to adjust the letter spacing of a title or a stand-alone word. When you increase the point-size of a word or use an all-capitalized word, any odd letter spacing is magnified. These odd spaces can occur between almost any pair of letters, but be especially alert when using "Ay" and "AW." Avoid adjusting the tracking or kerning more than five points. Both can be scaled positively (to add more air) or negatively (to condense). Adjusting more than five points either way may distort text. In Photoshop Elements, kerning for titles can be adjusted manually if each letter is created on its own layer. Use the Move tool to reposition the layers.

Leading

Leading is the typographic term for "line spacing." Leading can be adjusted to create an airy feel inside a block of text or, conversely, to condense it. Like fonts, standard leading is measured in points. Recommended leading is approximately ¼ to ⅓ of the point size of printed text (for example, the recommended leading between lines of 12 point text would be 3 to 4 points). Text printed in smaller point sizes requires more leading to enhance readability.

These pictures I snapped of my friend, Julie, are just so...well, Julie!

Tracking refers to the space between groups of letters (some might call those groups "words"). Deft tracking will enhance the readability of your text.

The space between lines of text is called leading. The term comes from the days of hand-operated printing presses, when actual pieces of lead were used between lines of type for spacing.

FAVORITE
unkerned

FAVORITE
kerned

The spacing between individual letters is called kerning. Letters such as "T," "W," "I," and "O" can visually throw off the spacing within a word, making it appear wonky. Use kerning to move letters closer or farther apart for visual balance. (Note the subtle differences between the unkerned and the kerned versions of "FAVORITE" above. The difference is obvious between the "VOR" and the "RI.")

Expert Adjustments

For the discriminating digital scrapbooker, no detail is too small to refine. The following are ways to finesse your text to an expert's level of perfection.

Widows

In typography, a "widow" is a word that sits by itself on the last line of text. To get rid of a widow, edit your text so that it is just a bit tighter and shorter. That will shift the last word (that widow) up to the line above. If that doesn't work, adjust the tracking of the entire body of text.

Hyphenation

Too many hyphens at the ends of lines in blocks of text create a visual distraction. In longer blocks of text, avoiding hyphens altogether is impossible. Alleviate hyphens at the end of a line of text by editing text to be concisely worded. Or, use a soft return (Shift-Return) to drop the entire word onto the next line. As a last measure, adjust the tracking of the entire block of text. Be sure never to double hyphenate on your pages (the hyphenation of an already hyphenated word). If you must hyphenate, be sure to hyphenate between syllables.

Proper Punctuation Characters

Did you know that there are two types of quotation marks? There are smart quotes and measurement (or prime) quotes. Smart quotes are the curly quotes used to denote quotations and dialogue. Measurement quotes are knife-straight and are used to denote units of measure. Knowing the difference will take your layouts from pretty cool to perfectly polished. Likewise, an ellipsis (the "dot, dot, dot" that signifies "etc." or "more to come") has a key command that allows it to be typed as a singular character rather than three separate but consecutive periods. See the table on p. 119 for special character keystrokes.

This all-capped title required a bit of kerning; otherwise, the spacing between the "I" and the "T" would have been too tight. You can adjust the kerning manually by creating a new text layer for each letter of your title. Select the layer and use the Move tool to reposition as desired.

Leah Blanco Williams

Types of Fonts
Three main categories

Fonts can be divided into many different categories, but scrapbookers need only worry about three. Each type has its own unique purpose, which, once understood, will make choosing the best fonts for your layout a snap.

Headline Fonts

A headline font has two goals: to draw the eye and impart a clear message. Headline fonts are an ideal choice for a title or for subheads that break up long journaling blocks. In your daily newspaper, the headline fonts are clean and distinct because of their size, boldness, and contrast with the text font. These fonts generally look best when sized 18 points (a point size is the length between the tallest ascender and longest descender found in a respective font) and higher. When choosing a headline font, pick one that is appropriate for the tone of your page. For ease, look for fonts that have equal letter spacing, because the font's large size will emphasize odd letter spacing.

Text Fonts

Crafted to be used in longer passages of text, these fonts are easily read at smaller point sizes (11 to 14 points is the "Goldilocks" size for body text—it is neither too big nor too small). Text fonts are clean and easy on the eyes. Serif fonts, which are characterized by the little "foot," or serif, at the base of the letter forms, are a good choice because the serifs connect letters and create a natural visual flow. If you choose a serif font for your journaling, consider using a sans serif (a font without the foot) for your title. It will provide a nice contrast. If you want to add spice to these basic fonts, try using italics, block, all capitals, reversed, and colored text for keywords within the passage.

serif

Fonts are available in two basic varieties: serif (left) and sans serif (right). Serif fonts have extenders on the end points of the letters. Sans serif fonts offer a cleaner, more modern look and are great for headlines, especially those composed of all caps.

Font Vocab

In order to understand a discussion of fonts, you should be familiar with very basic terms including:

- **X-height:** The height of a lowercase letter, which is determined relative to the lowercase letter "x."
- **Baseline**: The imaginary line that a font rests upon. Most are straight, but some fonts are characterized by bouncing or slanting baselines that affect the aesthetic quality of the words.
- **Ascenders and descenders:** These letter parts extend above the x-height (ascender) or descend below the baseline (descender).

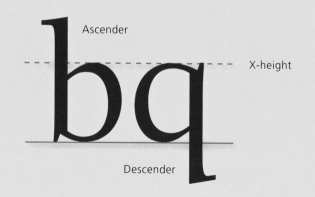

Great Headline and Text Font Families

Opt for members of these no-fail favorite font families when crafting a title and journaling for your layout.

- **Headline Fonts**

Bodoni POSTER
CASLON BOLD
COMIC SANS
Helvetica BLACK
IMPACT
Memphis Extra Bold
TRAJAN BOLD
Verdana Bold

- **Text Fonts**

Arial Narrow
Caslon
Egyptienne
Helvetica Roman
Novarese Book
Memphis Light
Times Roman
Palatino Roman
Univers Roman

This title, created with Impact font, which is a bold, sans serif font, accomplishes its job—it grabs the eye and holds the reader. The bold strokes and thickness of the letters contrast beautifully with the Jey font, chosen to accent the title. The journaling is clearly readable in Times New Roman.

I have always enjoyed watching my children discover new things. Watching Samantha learn how to use her hands was no exception. At 4 months old I would often catch her examining her hands, turning and flexing them. She quickly learned from there that she could grab things with her hands and, of course, put them in her mouth. I just love the intent look on her face as she learns something new. It makes me look forward to all the things I'm going to get to watch her learn over the years.

new worlds opened up when Samantha discovered toys.

Sheila Doherty

Specialty Fonts

For most, this is where the font fun comes in. They are the scripty, flirty, occasion-inspired, funny, goofy, and downright sassy sisters of the more practical headline and text fonts. Their history dates back to the middle of the 19th century, when type designers started creating alphabets with complex brush strokes, and decorative elements.

Ornamental fonts boast grand organic shapes and modern deco touches, while novelty fonts can appear balloon-like, chalked as if written on the blackboard, or stamped. When using these fonts, keep readability in mind. Most of them are going to look best at larger point sizes. Try them with shorter titles, to emphasize a single word in a title, or to accent keywords inside a journaling block.

Everything about the text on this page, from the title to the journaling block, says "laid back." The font set Beautiful and Beautiful Caps, with exaggerated ascenders and descenders, stretches out in lovely script on a beachy blanket of white. The journaling font, Copperplate Bold, adds excellent contrast.

Leah Blanco Williams

Extraordinary Ornamental and Novelty Fonts

Scrapbookers love the energy and emotion these fonts bring to pages. Featured here is just a small sampling of a vast world of choices.

Artefacts Bold

Bad Cabbage Primal

Banshee Script

Beatnik Regular

Curlz Regular

eurostile

Giddyup Standard

Immi Five O Five

LITHOS

ROSEWOOD

STENCIL

Wendy Medium

A ninja page like this called for a slew of novelty fonts (Insomnia, Stereofidelic, Cheapsake, EL & Font Gothic Violation). The fonts work together to convey child-like fun, blocky energy, and in-your-face defiance with irregular letter heights and artistic brush strokes.

Leah Blanco Williams

PlumBAE font is a lovely set of script letters that works exceedingly well for this quote. The artist was careful to use a larger point size and deeper line spacing to ensure readability. The gentle swoop of the font's ascenders and descenders provides contrast to the soft serif title font (TrajanBricks).

Sheila Doherty

The Right Font for Your Layout

Pairing up a font and a page

Font styles are so abundant that it is easy to feel stumped when choosing the right ones for your scrapbook page. Indecisive types and fontaholics are especially vulnerable to becoming overwhelmed. Fonts convey energy and personality as well as information. For that reason, the best starting point for selecting a font is to consider the layout you are constructing.

Determining the Mood

If you want your layouts to generate a response, then they should have a mood. Mood begins with the photos and journaling. What emotions do they evoke? Love? Happiness? Spirit? Adoration? Your font choice should reflect this mood. Consider the following when determining the mood for your page.

- **Subject Character:** How would you describe the personalities of those in the photo? Let their individual energies guide your font selection.
- **Theme:** Is the page documenting a special occasion such as a birthday or holiday? Thematic fonts can benefit many a page.
- **Formal or Informal:** Will your page be stately and refined or comfy and casual? Think script fonts for elegance and handwritten or comical fonts for casual.
- **Age Specific:** How old are the photo subjects? Select fonts that seem to correlate with your subject's age.
- **Period Specific:** If you are scrapbooking heritage photos or retro memories, you will find a wealth of fonts to help reflect days gone by.

Airplane is the name of the simple, chunky font used on this page, which seems to perfectly describe the way it bounces up and down on the baseline. It's a great choice for a page about a sweet young boy's innocent curiosity.

Shannon Taylor

Using Multiple Fonts

If one font is good, two or three can be GREAT on a scrap-book page. (Four, however, is over the top, and you'll want to put the brakes on your mixing and matching fun before your page becomes a mishmash of type.) The key to the successful mixing of type styles is to find fonts that work well together to convey the mood of the layout, while balancing and supporting each other. Unfortunately, there is no science to mastering the manipulation of type, but there are some guidelines. The more you work with type, the keener your sense of design will become. Keep in mind that your type treatment must be readable to serve its primary purpose.

Create Contrast

A successful mix of fonts relies on contrast, which can be achieved in several ways. The easiest is to mix a serif and sans serif font. You can also contrast with variations in size and color. Mixing fonts of different styles (such as a distressed typewriter font with a clean stencil font) is usually visually pleasing.

Unify the Styles

When selecting contrasting fonts to use on a layout, you must take care that the styles of your selections do not clash. Look for unifying elements in the fonts, such as line quality, decorative touches, or similarities in ascenders and descenders. If unity needs to be reinforced, alter your fonts so they are the same color.

Experiment!

Remember, while there are guidelines to mixing fonts, there are no rules. It's a wide world full of choice, so dive in and experiment until you begin to develop an eye for your own personal font style.

Diane Miller

This artist selected Franklin Gothic Heavy as the primary font for her page, using it for the journaling and also for the word "spirited" in the title. She then added the word "free" in a more whimsical and elegant font (Cherish). Complementing a heavy block font with a delicate script style creates a winning mix. To enhance the contrast, the fonts were printed in complementary colors—soft blue and an orange so muted it is almost peach.

Design With Text
Infusing text with style

Font selection is the first step in determining the typographical treatment on your scrapbook page. The way you manipulate it and where you place the type are of equal importance. We have been conditioned to think that the job of text is to provide information and, while it certainly does perform that task, it does much more. When formatted and placed strategically on a scrapbook page, the text actually becomes a part of the creative vision.

Text Indicates Hierarchy

The average scrapbook page contains three text elements: the title, journaling, and photo captions. When designing your page, assign these elements a degree of importance. When choosing type styles for each, do so in a way that communicates the prescribed priority.

- Determine the path along which you'd like the reader's eye to travel across the page. Then use the text elements to direct the eye. The text element deemed the most important should be the first stop for the eye.
- Prioritize via size, boldness, and visual weight. As a general rule of thumb, the dominant text element will be largest, boldest, and carry the most weight, but as you become more comfortable designing text, mix these determinants for varying effects. For example, create a supersized text element but scale back the visual weight to create a dominant element that is a subtle attention-getter.
- Clearly differentiate between all font types, but avoid too many sizes and too many visual weights. As when mixing fonts, the recommended number of sizes and weights is three.

Text Can Be the Central Focus

Compelling stories deserve to be detailed in extensive journaling. Avoid long lines of text by printing text in columns. Break the text into chunks and separate them with subheads or other page elements, such as a title or photo. House text on its own matted background to distinguish it from other elements.

Keep in mind that text also can point, wave, overlap, and spiral on a page for impact. Allow text to draw the eye to page elements that you consider worthy of extra focus.

The text hierarchy on this digital layout is easy to determine. The title, with its decorative font mix, size, and wonderful orange and blue color contrast, grabs the eye immediately. As the eye travels down the two photos, bullet points direct the eye to the left to read the journaling, which is emphasized by high color contrast (yellow on red).

Sheila Doherty

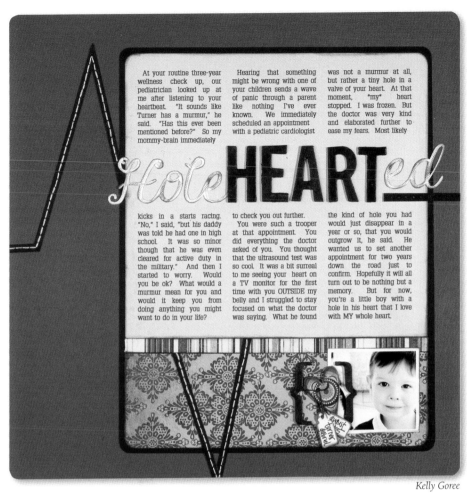

At your routine three-year wellness check up, our pediatrician looked up at me after listening to your heartbeat. "It sounds like Turner has a murmur," he said. "Has this ever been mentioned before?" So my mommy-brain immediately kicks in a starts racing. "No," I said, "but his daddy was told he had one in high school. It was so minor though that he was even cleared for active duty in the military." And then I started to worry. Would you be ok? What would a murmur mean for you and would it keep you from doing anything you might want to do in your life?

Hearing that something might be wrong with one of your children sends a wave of panic through a parent like nothing I've ever known. We immediately scheduled an appointment with a pediatric cardiologist to check you out further. You were such a trooper at that appointment. You did everything the doctor asked of you. You thought that the ultrasound test was so cool. It was a bit surreal to me seeing your heart on a TV monitor for the first time with you OUTSIDE my belly and I struggled to stay focused on what the doctor was saying. What he found

was not a murmur at all, but rather a tiny hole in a valve of your heart. At that moment, "my" heart stopped. I was frozen. But the doctor was very kind and elaborated further to ease my fears. Most likely the kind of hole you had would just disappear in a year or so, that you would outgrow it, he said. He wanted us to set another appointment for two years down the road just to confirm. Hopefully it will all turn out to be nothing but a memory. But for now, you're a little boy with a hole in his heart that I love with MY whole heart.

Kelly Goree

The story behind this scrapbook page is as endearing as it is long. Because of the length, the text was formatted into columns. Use the Type tool to create equal-sized text boxes and align them with equal spacing on your layout. Choose **View menu>Guides** to use grids to precisely position the text boxes with the Move tool. The columns make the journaling easier to read (as does the serif font, TypoSlabserif). To break an intimidating block of journaling, the title was strung through the middle of the journaling block.

Mary-Ann Buchanan, Photos: James Buchanan

This is a great example of how to use text as an attention-getter. The text spirals around the photo and emphasizes the focal point of the photo—the subject's eye. This is not a technique that you can re-create in Photoshop Elements. As you advance in digital scrapbooking, you may want to consider purchasing a vector-based application, such as Adobe Illustrator, which will allow you to manipulate text in all sorts of ways and then import the manipulated files into your image-editing program.

Text Can Be a Unifying Element

Great scrapbook layouts exhibit unity, or a sense that page elements have healthy relationships with one another. There is usually one page element that enhances this sense of unity. Text works exceptionally well as a unifier. It is easy to unobtrusively stretch text across elements and layouts, thereby helping to bridge gaps and connect elements.

Text Can Be a Design Element

Include text on your layout by incorporating it into a design element. Try using text to create patterned paper designs. Create a photo frame with text. Instead of conventional flower stems, build them with words. Insert text into the curves of a flourish. Run text along the waves or lines of a pattern. See the layout on p. 131 and the step-by-step illustration for how to create text shapes.

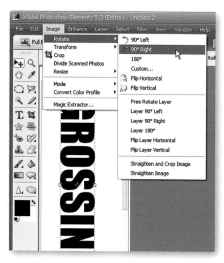

The title of this page frames the subject's face, directing attention to her expression. The rotated type slides down the page, bridging the photo to the overlapping page elements. To rotate type, choose the Type tool, click on the canvas, and type the text. Select the Type layer in the Layers palette and rotate 90 degrees right (choose **Image menu>Rotate> Layer 90° Right**). This title lettering was tweaked with Slight Emboss and Texture filters. The opacity was set to 5 percent. The result is text that looks like a traditional rub-on lettering accent.

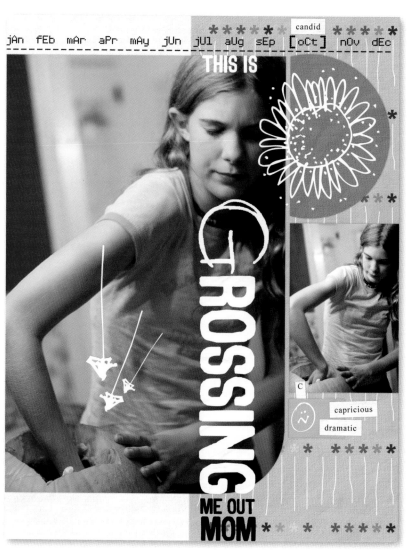

Tonya Doughty

See the layout on p. 131

DIGITAL DIVAS KNOW

Design vertical type by turning an entire word sideways rather than stacking the letters on top of each other. It's easier to read.

Text can easily be transformed into a design element. In this layout, text was placed inside a house. Use the Shape tool to create a guide for your text.

Leah Blanco Williams

Step 1

Select the Custom Shape tool from the Toolbox. Select the desired shape and color from the Options bar. Drag the tool across your canvas. Use the Move tool to resize and reposition the shape.

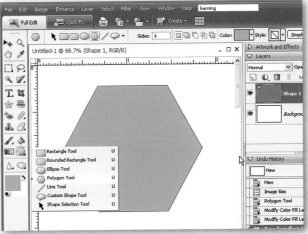

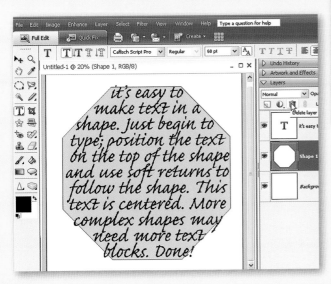

Step 2

Choose the Type tool from the Toolbox. Choose font, size, leading, and color from the Options bar. Click the Type tool where you want to begin typing over the shape. Elements will create a new type layer. Soft Returns (Shift-Return) are used to wrap the text. When finished, select the shape and hit Delete.

Type Tricks
Making type rock

Now that you have a foundation in working and designing with text, it's time to make it ROAR! On the pages that follow are a bevy of easy tried-and-true, oohed-and-ahhed-over text treatments. Use these examples as a springboard for your own creative exploration.

Layered Fonts

Layering two distinct styles of fonts is an excellent way to create contrast within your type design. The most popular choice is to layer an elegant script font on top of a block font. Use the block font as the base because it is bold and clear enough to support a second font. The delicate lines of the script font are so different from the block style that they appear to dance across the face of it. Layer different words or layer the same words for emphasis.

Text Wrap

A text wrap is a body of text that hugs another page element, most commonly a photo. Text wraps allow you to work around photos, titles, and embellishments, giving a layout a sense of unity. Inspiration for this technique is no farther than your coffee table. Grab your favorite magazine and look for advertisements that feature text saddling up to product images.

A light script font is layered over the outline of a blockier style to create a unique title for this page. Using the Type tool, choose a large block font (Chutzpah is used here) from the Options bar, and type the bottom word. Select a more delicate font (Hannibal Lecter is used here) to type the rest of the title. Use the Move tool to reposition the text as desired.

De Anna Heidmann

On the VERGE

be a queen. dare to be different. be a pioneer. be a leader. be the kind of woman who in the face of adversity will continue to embrace life and walk fearlessly toward the challenge. take it on! be a truth seeker and rule your domain, whatever it is your home, your office, your family with a loving heart.

be a queen. be tender. continue to give birth to new ideas and rejoice in your womanhood. my prayer is that we will stop wasting time being mundane and mediocre. we are daughters of god here to teach the world how to love.

it doesn't matter what you've been through. where you come from, who your parents are nor your social or economic status. none of that matters. what matters is how you choose to love. how you choose to express that love through your work. through your family. through what you have to give to the world. be a queen. own your power and your glory!

-oprah winfrey

Shannon Taylor

A text wrap allows you to work around other page elements. The easiest way to do this is to leave journaling for last. Insert text boxes next to images and then type in text. To get the text to hug the image, simply insert the Soft Returns (Shift-Return) where appropriate.

Reverse a Letter

Reversing a letter or word makes readers stop in their tracks while they struggle to understand "why." Why has the artist decided to flip text? The answer is that it gives the reader pause and prompts her to think about the page theme. It is a call to climb inside the layout, or inside the mind of the subject featured in the layout.

Change the Opacity

By reducing the opacity of a word, you soften the type and give it a ghostlike quality. The text no longer jumps out at you, but calls you to lean into the page. Less opaque text is more challenging to read, so use this type trick on oversized letters or when you plan to use the altered text as the foundation upon which another type treatment will be placed.

Angela Spangler

The single backward title word on this page is a perfect use of letter or word reversal. Backward text should be reserved for emphasizing keywords. Activate the Type layer you wish to reverse. Choose **Image menu>Rotate>Flip Layer Horizontal**.

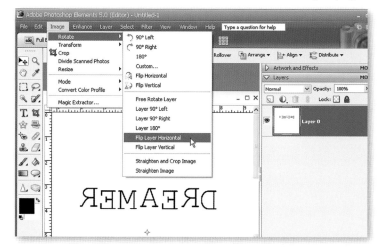

In our crazy,
fast-paced,
mile-a-minute
world, there
are a few
things
I know
with
absolute
certainty —
just how
very much
I love you
and that
I always
will.

Lisa Hoffer

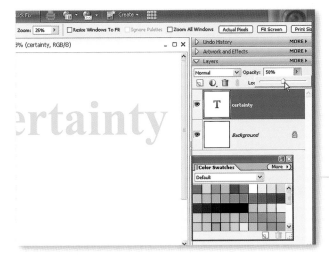

An oversized title leaves no guesswork as to the theme of this page. It can take the place of a page border when run either horizontally or vertically along the edge of a layout. These lowercase letters appear as windblown as the child herself, and the scaled back opacity creates a mood that is tentative. Activate the Type layer and adjust the opacity in the Layers palette. The default is set at 100 percent. Decrease the number until you reach the desired look.

DIGITAL DIVAS KNOW

Opacity is a terrific way to soften the color of a title. By reducing your opacity setting, your title blends with the background, reducing its presence on the page.

Create Drop Caps

Drop caps—oversized letters (cap is short for "capital") that herald the beginning of a paragraph—attract the eye and create a visual break in layout design. They add drama to a page. While drop caps can appear very upscale and elegant when used on wedding invitations and formal documents, they can be used with less formal text blocks (including scrapbook pages) when the font used is less ornate.

Sensitive child. Always a dignified person, at about age five, you became much more reserved, with an emerging ferocious temper.

Introspective one. You wait before you speak; observe before you act. Always a slight pause. And yet, your silence often hides deep roiling emotions.

Xiao Long. Born in the Year of the Dragon, the fortune teller told us that you would be highly intelligent, headstrong and stubborn, equally fierce and emotional. It will be our lifelong task to guide those traits into a good and productive life.

Wendy Chang

This page benefits from three drop caps, which also spell out the young boy's age. The letters begin the first word, which is a single adjective, of the three successive paragraphs. The large red letters tie together the red accents and red in the photo.

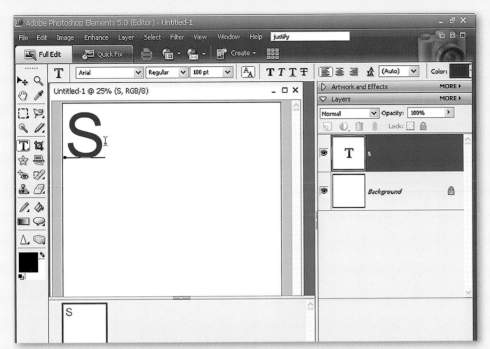

Step 1

To create an enlarged letter, choose the Type tool from the Toolbox. In the Options bar, determine the font, point size, type style, and color. Click on the canvas and type the letter; a new layer will be created. Use the Move tool to reposition the letter as desired.

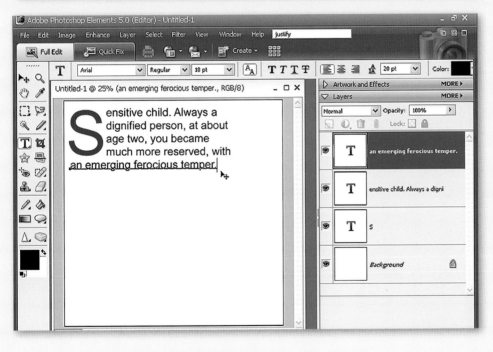

Step 2

Choose the Type tool and click on the canvas; type in the paragraph text and a new layer will be created. Use Returns as needed to create the desired line length. For this example, one text block sits to the right of the letter S; the last line is a separate text block positioned just below the enlarged letter. Use the Move tool to reposition or resize the text blocks or enlarged letter as desired.

DIGITAL DIVAS KNOW

There are several ways to create a drop cap. The easiest is to simply increase the point size or visual weight of the first letter, then adjust the tracking and/or kerning.

Fill Your Font With Color

Colored text can add energy, attract attention, emphasize a word, and affect the mood of a page. As a digital scrapbooker, you can creatively fill outline fonts with whatever color or colored pattern you choose. Be sure to carefully select your font choice when coloring inside the lines. Detailed and very slender fonts do NOT play well with color. Their stylized look already compromises readability.

Filling an outline font with a pattern that matches your layout palette is a wonderful way to unify a scrapbook page. Select a font that provides enough open space and be sure the holding lines of the font are wide enough to prevent the title from fading into the background.

Debbie Hodge

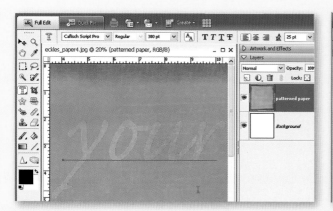

Step 1

To place a pattern behind an outline font, open a digital patterned paper file on a new layer. Choose the Horizontal Type Mask tool (hidden under the Type tool in the Toolbox) to type the title. As you type, a colored "mask" will appear over the entire layer. The text will be only slightly visible. If you wish to reposition the text, you must do so at this stage without selecting the Move tool; hold down the Ctrl (PC)/Cmd (Mac) key (a bounding box will appear) and drag to reposition.

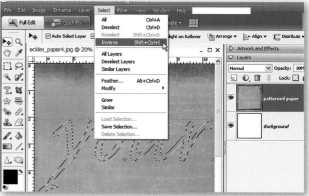

Step 2

Click on the Move tool and the text will become an active selection. To create the look on the layout above, choose **Select menu>Inverse** and hit the Delete key. Deselect the word by choosing **Select menu>Deselect**.

Angela Spangler

Brushes were used to fill in the title of this page. Brushes are a great way to add color, texture, pattern, and depth to letters.

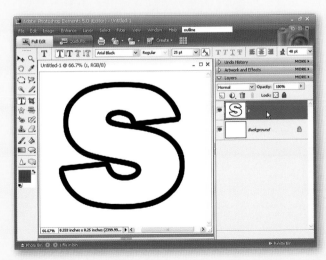

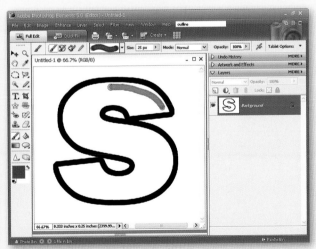

Step 1

Select the Type layer and simplify; in the Layers palette, choose **More>Simplify Layer**.

Step 2

Use the Paintbrush tool (adjust the brush size in the Options bar) to fill the letter with color by clicking on the layer and dragging the brush across.

Type on a Curve

Text can flow like a river down or across your page, or around photos and other layout elements. To make it happen, make your type curve. If your software does not offer this feature, see if you can warp text.

Highlight Key Words

Emphasizing certain words by highlighting the font or by creating a contrasting colored text box around the word adds punch to a layout. Carefully placed highlighted words can direct the eye to important elements on a layout, such as the photo or a piece of memorabilia.

This text waves down the side of the page, following the contour of the model's hair. This is a technique best accomplished with professional-grade graphics programs. In a pinch, the Text Warp tool can be used to distort text.

Michelle Godin

The highlighted words and phrases on this digital page create a visual ladder that guides the eye to the photo. Each highlighted word or phrase is created individually.

EVERY YEAR WE HEAD TO THE PUMPKIN
PATCH IN MORGAN HILL
EVERY YEAR WE PICK UP EVERY SINGLE
PUMPKIN OUT THERE
EVERY YEAR WE ARE ON THE LOOKOUT
FOR THE PERFECT ONE
EVERY YEAR WE END UP TAKING ONE
FOR EACH OF US
EVERY YEAR WE'RE HAVING LOTS OF FUN

Dagmar Nuemann

Step 1

Create a new layer and use the Rectangular Marquee tool to create a box for the typed word, then choose **Edit menu>Fill Selection**. When the dialog box appears, select Color to open the Color Picker. Select a color, click OK.

Step 2

Use the Type tool to create text on top of the box. Customize the text tool in the Options bar, then click on top of the colored box and begin typing. A new type layer will appear. Use the Move tool to reposition as desired.

Text Inside a Shape

Think inside the box...or circle, or triangle, star, or whatever you can draw. Placing your text in a shape can be done in some image-editing software programs.

If not, you can create the text element in another program, such as Adobe Illustrator or Microsoft Word®. See the steps below for creating this text with an image-editing program.

Text borders the photo montage and curves to follow a circular title element and airplane design. This advanced technique is a great way to challenge your digital skills.

Samantha Walker

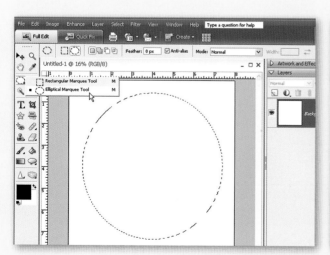

Step 1

Create a new layer and use the Elliptical Marquee tool to create a circle.

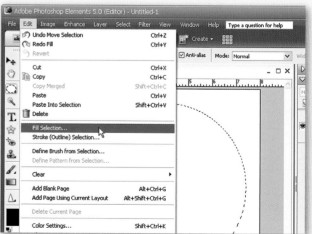

Step 2

From the Edit menu, select Fill Selection.

Step 3

A Fill Layer window will open and you can select foreground, background, black, white, or color. If you select color, the Color Picker window will open. Select the color you want and click OK. Then click OK in the Fill Layer box.

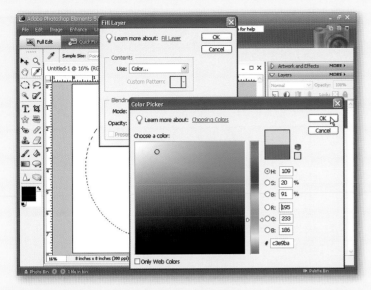

Step 4

Use the Rectangular Marquee tool to create a box. Move it over the circle so it cuts the circle in half (it's a good idea to turn on the grid; choose **View menu>Grid**). Click your Delete key to remove half the circle.

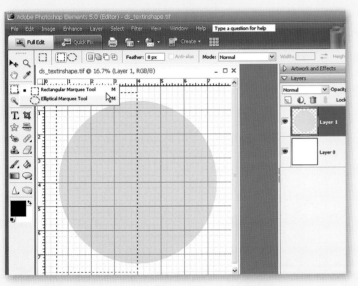

Step 5

Use the Type tool to type in your text. Use Soft Returns (Shift-Return) to create line breaks. Add spaces between words to make your lines fit the shape, if needed. When finished, delete the Shape layer.

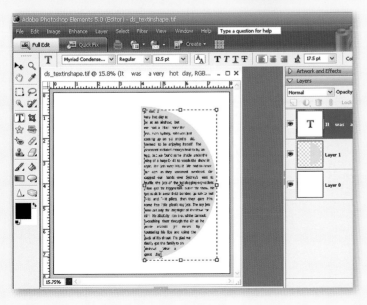

Make Your Words Speak
Writing tips and tricks

Every layout has a story, and telling it is an important part of scrapbooking. No matter how hard you try to remember them, details surrounding a particular event fade over time. You may forget names of neighbors, or your child's best kindergarten friend, or the exact hotel where you stayed on vacation. Feelings fade as well. They are never as poignant as they are in the immediate aftermath of the event. For these reasons, it is imperative to journal on your scrapbook pages.

Find and Polish Your Voice

Writing a first draft is difficult—any professional writer will tell you that. But tough as it may be, you need to slog through it until you have something that is complete enough to polish. You'll find the going easier if you are in the practice of writing daily. Daily writing in a journal keeps the wheels greased so you are ready to move forward when you want to add journaling to a piece of art. A personal journal also makes a wonderful place for you to record descriptive phrases and note writing styles used by authors you admire.

Spend some time with the photos you intend to use in order to get the words flowing. Write down words that the images inspire, or detail full-blown memories. Describe the feelings the photos stir. Allow the ideas to percolate for a while. When you return to them, organize them into a format for your page and then begin to write. Write the way you talk. Pretend you are describing the page subject to your best friend. The result will be full of detail in a fun, conversational tone that is inviting to read.

Edit Your Work

Polished text results from concisely written copy. Once you have completed your first draft, take another look at it with a critic's eyes. Ask yourself the following:

- **Do I have a clear focus?** Only include information pertinent to the topic you are honoring on your scrapbook page. Do not add unrelated information.
- **Have I included only the best information?** Edit your information. Include only the best anecdotes, the best illustrative points, the best quotes, and the best moments.
- **Have I been redundant?** If you have essentially said the same thing more than once, delete repetitive information.
- **Did I use the active voice?** Using verbs that clearly express action shortens text and makes prose powerful.
- **Are my sentences short?** It's tempting to pack a sentence with information, but avoid it. Strive for sentences that express one idea at a time. Complex sentences are only used when two ideas are so strongly related that they must be connected.

Two simple lists erupt with detail about these two pup pals. The highlighted words in these lists were created exactly like the highlighted words on p. 141.

Heidi Schueller

Journaling Tricks

If you want to shake things up a bit, try some alternative journaling styles. Stretching yourself as a writer will make you increasingly comfortable with the written word and keep your layouts fresh and interesting. Below is a list of journaling treatments that are fun and very easy to master.

- **Newspaper-Style:** Get the story! Find out the "who, what, when, where, whys and how" of the situation. Once these facts are gathered, write your own story, complete with a snappy headline.
- **Highlights:** If long-winded storytellers leave you rolling your eyes, then a simple list of the milestones, achievements, or juicy details is the way to go.
- **A letter:** For an emotionally charged page, treat the journaling as a letter. Salute your subject, tip over your heart, and let it spill.
- **An Interview:** A formal interview allows you to compile enough information to create a comprehensive story. Come to the interview prepared with a list of questions, but allow yourself to go with the conversational flow. Recording the interview allows you to focus and interact more freely with your subject.
- **Quotes and Lyrics:** If you believe that someone else can say it better, then use their words. Quotes, poems, and lyrics make wonderful journaling on scrapbook pages.
- **Lists:** You can create a list about lessons, reasons why you love thee, favorites, memories, gifts, fears or accomplishments, and anything else you deem interesting.

Quoted questions relay a child's enthusiastic curiosity and a grandfather's enormous range of wisdom. Using real dialogue makes journaling a snap. Keep a small notebook in your purse to capture conversational gems. The font Bernard MT Condensed chosen for this title is a simple serif headline font, but because of its enhanced size and weight, you can practically hear the child exclaim, "Grandpa!" The second font, Artistamp Medium, used for the journaling, makes the lettering look as if it has been hand-stamped.

Christine Brown

flower girl

Avery's first bluebonnet picture

DATE: 03-24-2007

Heidi Knight

Digital Backgrounds and Accents

What could be more exciting than creating your own backgrounds and accents from scratch—a perfect canvas for your photos. Original backgrounds and accents assure that nothing stands in the way of your ultimate creative vision.

Over the course of the previous chapters, you've come a great distance as a digital scrapbooker, having organized your digital crop station and becoming much more familiar with your equipment. You built your first digital layout, developed a deeper understanding about page design, and learned to edit and alter images like a pro. Any challenges you might have encountered with text have been overcome. It is now time to push the envelope and explore new concepts.

As you begin this chapter, think of yourself as a master's student in digital scrapbooking. The platform of knowledge you've established will allow you to move forward with the confidence to experiment on your own. Congratulations!

Getting the Look
Digitally Reproducing Popular Techniques

In this chapter you'll build on your knowledge of previously learned digital techniques and tool applications. You will also explore techniques that can be mixed and matched to create a variety of creative results.

What defines your personal scrapbook style? A personal style draws its uniqueness from your favorite colors, textures, type styles, voice, photographic perspectives, shapes, and patterns. If you pinpoint what you are most drawn to, you'll determine the techniques you'll want to learn to finesse. The frame you will learn how to create on p. 170 can be stamped, distressed, or painted to match your own design sensibilities. Along with the photography and journaling, it is the customizing of digital elements that will make your scrapbook pages completely unique.

Use These Tools

As you venture into the world of original backgrounds and accents, it is guaranteed that you will fall in love with a few digital tools with which you are already familiar. The key to all of these tools and to digital scrapbooking in general is this: Experiment with reckless abandon.

The following principal tools are covered: the Artwork and Effects palette, Brush tool, Eraser tool, and Shape tools. The Artwork and Effects palette gives you one-touch texture, dimension, and way-cool filters and effects. Open a photo and simply spend some time applying these filters and effects. Some of them, such as the Gaussian Blur filter, have their own dialog boxes, which will allow you to customize the result.

Brushes are fantastic and so easy to use. Almost anything can become a brush. With brushes, the Options bar will be your best friend, allowing you to customize any brush in myriad ways. The Eraser tool works just like a brush. You won't believe all of the incredible looks you can get by *erasing* parts of an image with a customized brush tip.

The Shape tools make building elements a breeze. There are existing shapes that you can use or you can build your own. Then you can apply any digital embellishing technique to your heart's content.

Save Your Creations

You'll find that creating your own custom papers and accents requires an investment of time and energy. As such, saving the work makes a lot of sense. You will definitely want to reuse the fruits of your labors on subsequent pages. Follow these guidelines to successfully save your custom-created backgrounds and accents.

- It's a good idea to save a backup native-format, layered version of backgrounds and accents so you can alter them in the future, should you wish.

- Another option for finished backgrounds and final layouts is to save a final flattened version as a TIFF file. This file-format is "lossless," meaning no data will be lost when the file is opened again and again. When you want to place a TIFF background on a new scrapbook page, simply copy and paste the file as is. TIFF is also a good choice if you want to use the file you created in another application such as a word-processing program.

- If space on your computer is at a premium and you do not have a CD or DVD burner to archive your creations, use the JPEG format. This format produces a high-quality file that takes up considerably less memory than a TIFF or PSD file. The drawback is that JPEG files will lose quality when opened again and again.

- Save accents as PNG files (pronounced "ping"). PNG format utilizes lossless compression, meaning the file will be compressed without losing data or reducing image quality. The steps you take to save the accent also will result in a transparent background layer, making it unnecessary to select the accent and delete the background each time you use it. Any curved lines or drop shadows also will be preserved. The size at which you create an accent will be dependent on use. For example, if you create a frame and can envision wanting to use the frame for an 8" x 10" photograph, make the frame 8" x 10". You can always reduce the file without fear of losing image quality; the same cannot be said about enlarging.

Hold my hand for a *moment* and my heart for a *lifetime*

This tender photo was captured in Disneyland. Mimi and Papa watched the babies while we rode rides with the older kids. Papa looked like he was in heaven holding a sleeping Avery. Her tiny hand in his big hand, safe and protected. She looked just as content as he was in that beautiful moment.

Avery & Papa

March. 2007

Heidi Knight

Custom digital accents are easy to create. Several, including the stitching, tag, and photo corner, exist on this page. To see how each was created, flip to pp. 167, 171, and 173, respectively, for detailed instructions.

DIGITAL DIVAS KNOW

Remember, delete the Background layer (to preserve transparency) when saving a PNG file. If the embellishment is large and has a lot of layers with effects, merge those layers together (don't flatten) to manage the file size. If you flatten the image, you will lose its transparency.

Digital Painting

Digital painting can be as simple as applying a few digital brush strokes of paint across a digital canvas or as involved as creating a digital masterpiece. The digital painter has a few advantages over the traditional painter. First, she can delete mistakes (**Edit menu>Undo**) and, if she changes her mind about the deletion, she can reimpose the stroke (**Edit menu>Redo**). She can also paint in layers for a dizzying array of results.

With digital painting, your tools are the Color Picker, Paint Bucket tool, brushes, and erasers. You also have a veritable treasure chest of dimensional and painterly special effects and filters from which to choose.

Color Picker

The Color Picker is your painter's palette; use it to select color for your brushes as well as the Paint Bucket. Click the Foreground/Background Color icon on the Toolbox to see it. Inside the dialog box are two stacked rectangular color boxes. The top box represents the new color you have picked and the bottom box represents the existing color. The large box is known as the color field; it shows the new color's full range of brightness and saturation. Inside the color field is a circular pointer. Move it left to right to adjust saturation or move it up and down to adjust brightness. Just to the right of the large box is a slider to change the hue. You can also select colors based on numerical values of HSB (hue, saturation, brightness) or RGB (red, green, blue). If you click on the small box in the bottom left corner, only Web colors will be available. When you move the pointer outside of the Color Picker dialog box, it changes to the Eyedropper tool; use the Eyedropper to sample a color from your canvas or photo (the sample will appear in the top color box inside the Color Picker dialog box; manipulate the color as desired). Click OK to apply changes.

Paint Bucket

The Paint Bucket tool should be used when you want to fill a large area with color, such as a layer. You can also use it to fill an area that has a high-contrast border. Use the Options bar to customize the Paint Bucket. You can fill the bucket with either a color or a pattern. To control how precise the Paint Bucket spreads color, adjust the Tolerance. Tolerance is the difference in value between neighboring pixels. The higher the Tolerance, the more pixels that will be affected. If the Tolerance is set at 100 percent, the Paint Bucket tool will fill the entire selection; if the Tolerance is set at 25, the color range will be much more specific. Anti-alias smooths any edges of your color fill if clicked. Clicking Contiguous will only fill pixels similar in tonal and color value that are directly adjacent to the selected area. To affect all layers simultaneously, choose Use All Layers in the Options bar.

Brush Tools

Use the Brush tools when you want to paint in strokes. Recall that once you choose a Brush tool, hundreds of brush styles exist in the drop-down menu on the Options bar. Brushes can be customized and even created to achieve your desired effect. See pp. 104 - 107 to review these wonderful tools.

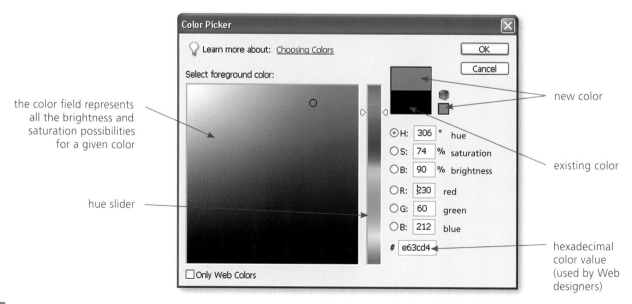

the color field represents all the brightness and saturation possibilities for a given color

hue slider

new color

existing color

hexadecimal color value (used by Web designers)

The artist used short, random brush strokes on a solid-color background to achieve the colorwash appearance of this paper. See below for detailed instructions.

Leah Blanco Williams

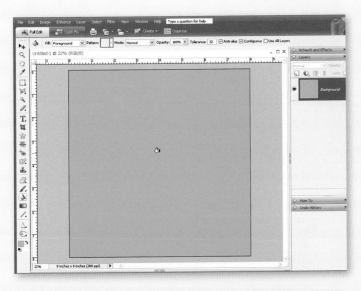

Step 1

Open a new document. Click on the Foreground box to open the Color Picker dialog box and choose a color. Use the Paint Bucket tool to fill the Background layer with the chosen color.

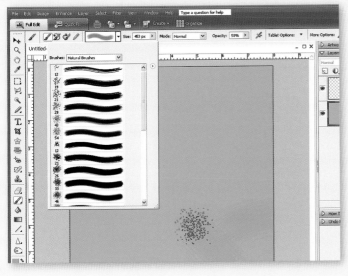

Step 2

Create a new layer and open the Color Picker to choose a color. Choose the Brush tool and optimize as desired in the Options bar. (For this paper, use the Stipple 54 Pixels brush from the Natural Brushes library in the Options bar.) The opacity was reduced to 50 percent. Drag randomly in short strokes across the canvas to paint.

To create the background shown in this layout and below, the artist used three of the Photoshop Elements Wet Media brushes (select the Brush tool and then scroll through the brush styles in the drop-down menu on the Options bar; here, brushes 5, 9, and 45 were used). For a paint-splatter effect, adjust the Spacing, Hue Jitter, and Scatter options in the Brush Options palette (to view, click the More Options paintbrush icon in the Options bar).

Leah Blanco Williams

DIGITAL DIVAS KNOW

You can use the Impressionist Brush tool (hidden under the Brush tool) to transform a photo into a Monet or a Cézanne. Open the image, choose the tool, and customize on the Options bar. Drag the brush across your image and watch as the metamorphosis occurs. Brush sizes between 6 and 10 pixels are recommended for fascinating results.

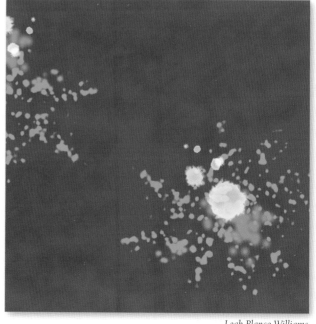

Leah Blanco Williams

01/2007

DOWNTOWN DISNEY DINING

WITH PLENTY OF TIME TO SPARE
BEFORE MY RED EYE FLIGHT THRU PITTSBURGH,
I DECIDED TO TREAT MYSELF TO A
HEARTY MEXICAN MEAL
AT TORTILLA JO'S IN DOWNTOWN DISNEY.
IT WAS ENOUGH TO KEEP MY BELLY SATISFIED
THE WHOLE JOURNEY HOME AND THE MORNING AFTER!

Leah Blanco Williams

Wet Media brushes also were used to create this background, but in this case part of the background was erased to create grungy edges. Wet Media 39 was used to create the color wash effect. Then, the Eraser tool was chosen and customized with the Wet Media 74 tip in the Options bar. The tool was dragged across the upper left and lower right corners.

Leah Blanco Williams

Digital Patterns

There are many ways to create patterned backgrounds in Photoshop Elements. Use an existing pattern from the program, a photo, a selected portion from a photo, a scanned image (such as your child's artwork) or texture (such as the examples shown on p. 33), a custom or pre-made digital accent, a digital brush pattern, or an original digital shape or doodle.

Create Patterns

The easiest way to fill a canvas with a pattern is with the Paint Bucket tool. Choose the tool and, in the Options bar, choose Pattern from the Fill drop-down menu and click the arrow to open the Pattern Picker. Choose the desired pattern and click on the canvas.

You can also use the Pattern Stamp tool, which is hidden beneath the Clone Stamp tool, to create paper with a mix of patterns. It's also perfect for creating a background with only a partial pattern. Like your Brush, Eraser, and Clone Stamp tools, the Pattern Stamp can be customized in the Options bar with different brush styles and sizes, and you can also manipulate opacity levels to reduce the intensity of the pattern. Click and drag the tool on your canvas to paint with the Pattern Stamp tool.

Download Patterns

You can load new patterns into Photoshop Elements. Search the Internet for "free fill patterns" to download.

Once downloaded, drop the files into the pattern folder on your hard drive (**Photoshop Elements>Presets> Pattern**). When using them, you may have to Simplify the layer in order to perform some edits. If the downloaded pattern file is a PNG format, you won't need to Simplify.

Repeating Patterns

Repeating motifs, whether photos, scanned images, or digital accents, can be used to create patterns that fill entire canvases. You can also use them to make a rhythmic border accent on an otherwise solid or textured background. Vary the scale of the repeated motif for interesting results. For example, surround a supersized motif with smaller versions in various sizes. Repeating patterns can also be created from a portion of a photo. Enlarge and crop images to develop interesting perspectives and textures. Experiment with the orientation of the image. See how rotating or flipping an image might affect the resulting pattern.

To create the pattern, select your background color and then either drag and drop (Elements 5.0) or copy and paste (**Edit menu>Cut; Edit menu>Paste**) from an image file onto a new layout. You can also create a brush from your image (see pp. 106 - 107) to repeatedly stamp the pattern on your layout. To assist in exact placement of the motif, turn on the Rulers (**View menu>Ruler**) and Grids (**View menu>Grids**); to customize the grid, choose **Edit menu>Preferences>Grid**.

Step 1

Create a new 12" x 12" canvas. Fill a new layer with color (**Edit menu>Fill Selection> Color**). In the Layers palette, scale back the opacity to the desired effect.

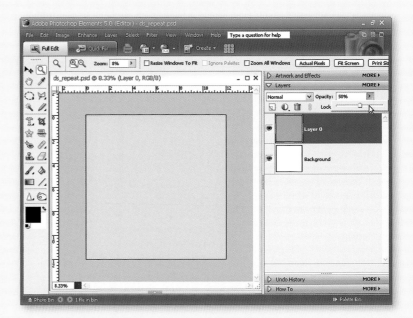

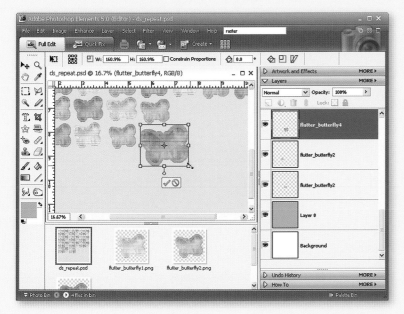

Step 2

Choose the motif that you wish to repeat (here we've used flutter_butterfly1, 2, 4 from the Flutter kit on the CD). Copy the embellishment (**Edit menu>Copy**). Click on your layout and choose **Edit menu>Paste**. The butterfly will appear on a new layer with a bounding box. Resize and reposition the butterfly as desired; click on the green checkmark to confirm. Add additional butterflies until your page is filled.

Shannon Taylor

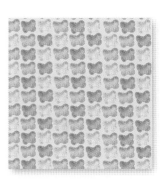

The butterfly-patterned paper above was created by repeating a digital butterfly element from the Flutter kit on the CD included with this book. The original paper is 12" x 12", but was resized to 8" x 8" for the layout to the left.

Photographic Patterned Paper

While any photo can be used to create background papers, those that feature a lot of texture, pattern, and/or color work best. Branch-filled forest scenes, cobblestone sidewalks, a freshly cut lawn, pebbled paths, dappled sunlight through leaves, clouds, doors, rosettes, and interesting façades all result in textural images that can be manipulated for excellent creative results. Keep a library of photos with strong potential.

When taking photos, keep in mind that you'll want to enlarge the images to create 12" x 12" or even 8" x 8" papers. Set your digital camera's file size so that the resulting resolution will permit enlargements that won't suffer loss of quality. Save cropping for last; the digital manipulation will determine which part of the image is worth keeping.

Manipulations can bring out alluring aspects of the photo or change it so significantly that it becomes an abstract. Decide if you want to enhance your selected image with color, texture, or both. Adjust the tonal values and saturation levels to alter the color. Tweaking brightness and contrast emphasizes the texture, as will Noise, Faux Finish, and Outline filters.

Step 1

The original photo, near right, was lightened. Choose **Enhance menu>Adjust Lighting>Brightness/Contrast**; in the dialog box, drag the Brightness slider for the desired effect.

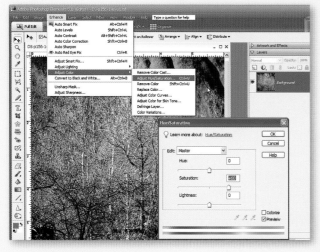

Step 2

To create a jewel-toned and highlighted palette, as in the image to the right, start by adjusting color saturation. Choose **Enhance menu>Adjust Color>Adjust Hue/Saturation**; in the dialog box, drag the Saturation slider for the desired effect.

Step 3

To add more variety to the image, alter individual colors in the Hue/Saturation dialog box (individual colors are found under the Master drop-down menu); drag sliders as desired for each color and click OK.

Step 4

You can apply a filter to create an abstract effect (here, we've applied **Filter menu>Pixelate>Facet**). To soften the image, choose **Filter menu>Blur>Gaussian Blur**.

Blur Filters

Photographic patterned papers can benefit from Blur filters. Apply these filters to an entire image or a selection to add a little motion, soften edges, and create cool effects.

Blur: This softens hard edges. It works well when there is too much contrast between the foreground and background.

Blur More: This works exactly like the Blur filter, but with more intensity. Therefore, you might have more success in applying it to selected areas of an image.

Gaussian Blur: This gives you the most control over your desired effect. When you choose this filter, a dialog box will appear with a slider that affects the amount of blur.

Motion Blur: Use this filter to imply kinetic energy in your photo. Use it to show movement or mimic panning a camera.

Radial Blur: You have the option to produce a "spin" or "zoom" blur, which either blurs everything into a cyclone or blurs it with magnification, respectively.

Smart Blur: If you simply want to soften an image or add a slight blur, choose the Smart Blur, which allows you to set the distance of the blur (Blur Radius) and the degree of pixels to be blurred (Threshold).

Digital Pattern Mixing

Create a mix of geometrics, botanicals, and other patterns for a truly interesting background. Start with a favorite pattern and then add three or four supporting prints. Make sure the base colors of your mix match (for example, all backgrounds should be either white or cream, etc.) and that the patterns share similar colors. To prevent the pattern from becoming static, add variety in scale and texture. For depth, filters and special effects (such as blurs) can be employed and opacity levels can be adjusted.

Sheila Doherty

To ensure a no-fail pattern mix, opt for patterns that originate from the same digital kit. Patterned papers from the City Beat digital kit on the CD included with this book were used to create this mix.

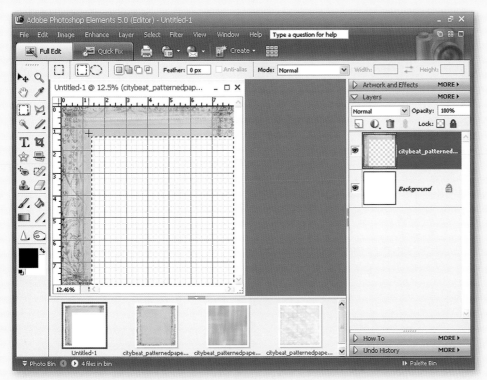

Step 1

Open a new document and turn on Rulers (**View menu>Rulers**) and Grids (**View menu>Grids**) to help with exact placement. Open desired paper (for this example, choose citybeat_patternedpaper1 from the City Beat kit on the CD). Copy (**Edit menu>Copy**) and paste (**Edit menu>Paste**) onto the canvas. Choose the Rectangular Marquee tool to select the area to be deleted; hit Delete. Choose **Select menu>Inverse** and hit Delete.

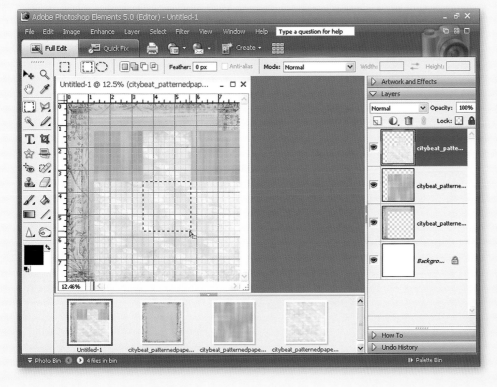

Step 2

Copy and paste additional papers as desired (here we used citybeat_patterned paper2 and citybeat_patternedpaper3). Use the Move tool to resize and reposition these two papers to fit in the void left by the blue paper. To create the block pattern with these two papers, select the top paper layer and use the Rectangular Marquee tool to select blocks; hit Delete and the paper below will show through. Hide the Background layer and choose **Layers palette>More>Merge Visible**. Save as a TIFF or JPEG by choosing **File menu>Save As**.

Digital Stamping

Traditional scrapbookers have always loved rubber stamping, and it is very easy for the digital scrapbooker to create the same coveted looks. The versatile Brush tool (see pp. 104 - 107 for more information) is the digital scrapbooker's rubber stamp, allowing her to apply swirling doodles, distressed line imagery, and other accents that have the look of hand stamping to layouts. Brushes make it easy to repeat patterns, alter the angle of the image, and execute precise placement.

The easiest way to use brushes for digital stamping is to use the existing Photoshop Elements brush styles. The Pen Pressure and Special Effects brush sets are great choices. You can customize them in the Options bar to achieve your desired effect. You also can create new brushes. For example, you can create a brush from an image, such as a flower, to use as a stamp. Or, if you own traditional rubber stamps, stamp the image onto a sheet of paper (for maximum contrast, use the darkest ink possible on white paper), scan it, and create a custom brush from the digital image (see p. 106 - 107 for instructions).

When you stamp digitally, the stamped images appear on the layer you select. It's a good idea to create a new layer for stamping. If you really want control over the size and positioning of each individual stamp, create a new layer for each. You can also apply dimensional layer effects to stamps on their own layers; use Bevels (in the Artwork and Effects palette) to create looks such as embossing.

The stamped designs on this digital patterned paper were created with a Photoshop Elements brush called Sunflower. It can be found in the brush style library in the Options bar under the Pen Pressure brush set.

Leah Blanco Williams

This digital stamping is the result of the Scattered Maple Leaves brush that can be found in the Default Brushes brush set. The colorful look was achieved by stamping the brush pattern on several different layers. The colors were chosen with the Eyedropper tool from papers in the Rio kit on the CD included with this book.

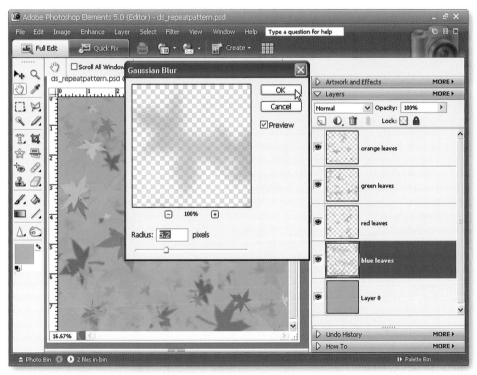

The depth in this design was created by using a smaller brush size on the lower layers as well as a higher blur (**Filter menu>Blur>Gaussian Blur**) and lower opacity setting. The top layer features larger brush sizes with no blur and little opacity.

DIGITAL DIVAS KNOW

Use clip art and illustrations to create custom digital brushes. Companies such as Dover Publications offer royalty-free clip art CDs and books filled with illustrations for crafters to use. Download or scan the art and follow the steps on pp. 106 - 107 to create a brush.

Digital Distressing

Distressing an element gives it a comfortably worn and weathered appearance. There is a variety of distressed looks, from verdigris and rusted to sanded and torn, and there are a number of ways to achieve them. A traditional scrapbooker's distressing toolbox includes sandpaper, brown and black stamping ink, steel wool, a stipple brush, chalks, and sponges, which she uses to stain, buff, tear, and roughen paper. Texture and dimension are added with chalks, sponged ink, and paint. The digital scrapbooker can achieve the same looks, relying on brush sets, the Eraser tool, and filters.

The most popular distressing brushes are the Dry Media and Wet Media brush sets, but explore the brush library for unexpected finds. For example, Faux Finish brushes can be used to apply fantastic texture to backgrounds and elements. The Eraser tool can create the illusion of torn edges on digital paper, photos, and paper elements, such as digital paper flowers. Experiment with filters, such as the Artistic, Brush Stroke, and Noise filters, for one-step distressing; filters are found in the Filter menu and in the Artwork and Effects palette. Try effects such as Sandpaper, Rusted Metal, and Asphalt (also found in the Artwork and Effects palette) to transform a paper or object on a layer.

Angela Spangler

Digital distressing was achieved in several ways on this layout. First, a sheet of grungy white paper creates the background (rio_solidpaper4 on the CD). Torn digital paper helps anchor the photo (see pp. 163 - 165 for instructions). A distressed font helps round out the page.

Step 1

Open a paper on a new layer (here we've used rio_solidpaper3 from the CD). Choose the Rectangular Marquee tool to select a strip from the paper, choose **Select menu>Inverse**, and hit Delete. The strip of paper will remain. Deselect (**Select menu>Deselect**).

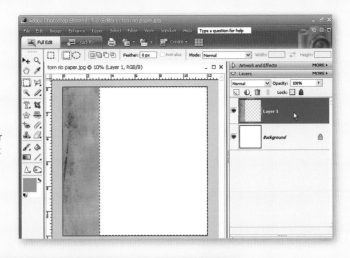

Step 2

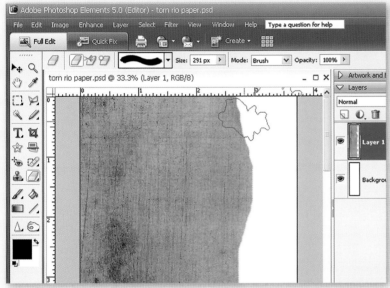

To create the torn edge, choose the Eraser tool and customize it in the Options bar so that the brush tip has a rough edge (here we used the Chalk 17 Pixels brush from the Default preset library). Drag it along the edge of the paper strip. Push the Ctrl key (Mac: Cmd) while clicking on the layer's thumbnail icon to select the torn paper. Choose **Select menu>Inverse** and hit Delete to erase any stray pixels.

Step 3

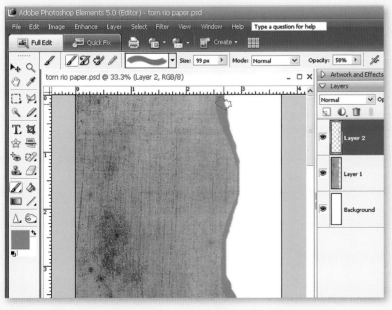

To give the torn edge texture, choose **Select menu>Inverse** to reselect the torn paper. Choose the Brush tool and customize as desired. Create a new layer and drag the brush along the "torn" edge. Deselect.

continued on p. 164

Step 4

Apply the Heavy Noisy filter (**Artwork and Effects palette>Layer Styles>Inner Glows>Simple Noisy**) to texturize the dark blue layer of the torn edge. Double-click on the starburst icon to customize the glow if desired.

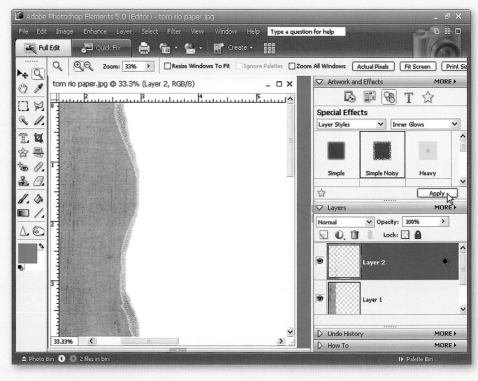

Step 5

Select the torn paper layer and add a drop shadow for dimension (**Artwork and Effects palette>Layer Styles>Drop Shadows >Low**). Double-click on the starburst icon to customize the shadow as desired.

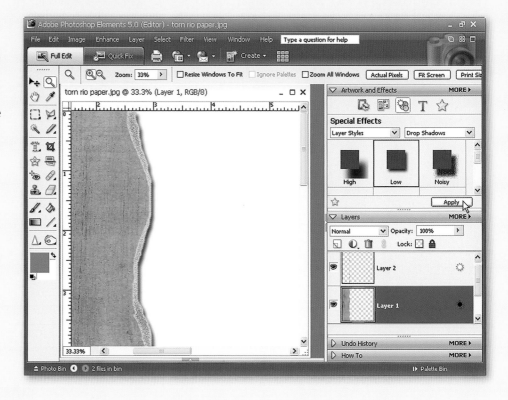

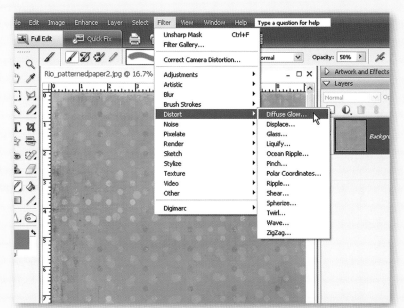

Bonus Distressing Technique

This sheet of paper (rio_patternedpaper2, from the Rio kit on the CD) was distressed using just one filter (**Filter menu> Distort>Diffuse Glow**).

Original Paper

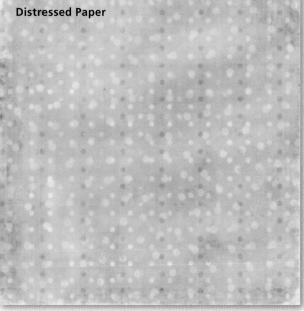

Distressed Paper

DIGITAL DIVAS KNOW

Don't limit yourself to scrapbooking Web sites when looking for distressing brushes. Search the Internet for "Photoshop Brushes" and you will be amazed at all of the wonderful brushes available for downloading at reasonable prices.

Point-and-Click Embellishments
Creating your own accents

Even though you have all the digital knowledge necessary to create any accent you desire, it's always best to begin with a simple project. The accents that follow are easy to re-create and to customize to your liking using many of the techniques with which you are already familiar.

Digital Stitching

Digital stitching fools the eye, prompting admirers to insist, "But that page MUST be real. It has stitching!" Stitching provides texture, a handcrafted touch, and often that little "something" your layout calls for to be complete. The three most basic stitches are the straight stitch, zigzag stitch, and cross-stitch, all of which can be created using the Brush tool. Choose a brush tip based on texture—you can create neat stitches or rough-edged stitches—and customize as desired. Creating digital stitches with a brush will allow you to create a repeating stitch pattern with the simple click of the mouse. Adjust the size, shape, and angle of the stitch in the Brush Dynamics palette. Simple modifications to the angle of the stitch brush allow you to create waving or spiraling stitches. (For more information regarding how to create brushes and brush sets, please see pp. 104 - 107.)

You can use the Line tool to draw a stitch and then create a brush from it as well. The Line tool is found hidden under the Custom Shape tool in the Toolbox. In the Options bar, you can determine the weight, or thickness, of the line as well as the color.

If you add stitches to your layout as their own layer, you can easily add texture and dimension to them. Refine your stitches with drop shadows and experiment with the shadow's lighting, angle, distance, and width. You can also apply bevels and/or filters to give the stitches added texture.

This detail from this scrapbook page (p. 149) shows effective use of digitally created stitching. The stitches, created with the Brush tool, were colored and treated with effects for dimension and realism.

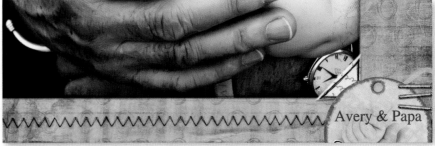

Heidi Knight

Step 1

To create your basic stitch, choose the Brush tool and customize it in the Options bar. Click and drag the brush to create your desired stitch, using grids (**View menu>Grids**) as your guide.

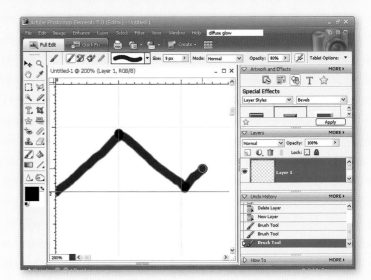

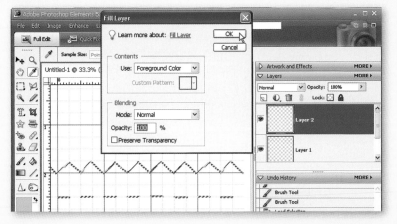

Step 2

Select the stitching; hold down the Ctrl key (Mac: Cmd) and click on the stitching layer's thumbnail icon. Choose **Edit menu>Fill Selection>Color>OK**.

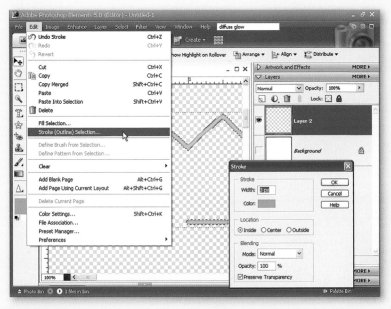

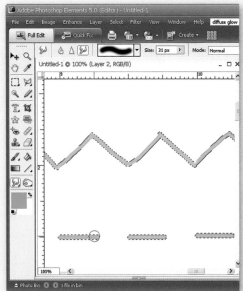

Step 3

To add dimension, outline the stitch with color. Choose **Edit menu> Stroke (Outline) Selection** and pick a slightly darker shade of the fill color; opt for an "Inside" fill and click OK.

Step 4

Use the Smudge tool (the finger icon in the Options bar) to blend the stroke into the middle area; this creates a bevel-like effect without any harsh shadows.

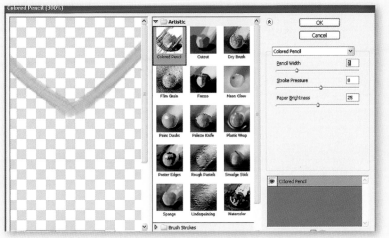

Step 5

To mimic the texture of thread, choose **Filter menu> Artistic>Colored Pencil**; in the dialog box, adjust the sliders to the desired effect and click OK. If desired, add a drop shadow (**Artwork and Effects palette>Layer styles>Drop Shadows>Low**); click on the starburst icon to customize. To add stitching holes, create a new layer and arrange below the stitches layer, choose the Brush tool (in the Options bar, adjust the size to be slightly larger than the one used to create the stitching), and click on each corner of each individual stitch.

Digital Chipboard

Chipboard is the brown, fibrous, cardboard-like paper that backs a notepad. Scrapbookers love chipboard because it can be used to add lightweight dimension to pages. The digital scrapbooker can create all the effects of chipboard in a few simple steps.

Use the Custom Shape tool to create your chipboard accents. The Custom Shape tool has shapes in the drop-down menu on the Options bar. Hidden under this tool are several other tools. The other tools allow you to draw your own shapes.

When using a Shape tool, the icons in the Options bar allow you to do the following: 1) create a new shape;

2) add to a shape; 3) subtract from a shape; 4) intersect a shape (this creates a shape from only the areas where the shapes overlap); and 5) combine shapes that overlap into one contiguous shape. Choose the appropriate icon before drawing your shape.

Every shape you create will exist on its own layer. These are called Shape layers, and they will need to be simplified if you plan on applying filters or special effects to them. Activate the layer and click the Simplify button.

You can also create chipboard shapes from photos and digital patterned papers. Use a Selection tool to isolate an area in the photo or paper and apply effects for dimension (see the step-by-step at right).

Any shape can be turned into a digital chipboard accent. This digital chipboard flower was created with a flower motif from a piece of digital patterned paper on your CD. See the steps on the right to re-create your own.

Sheila Doherty

Step 1

Open a piece of digital patterned paper on its own layer (here we've used rio_patternedpaper4 from the CD). Use the Crop tool to resize the paper so that only one flower exists on the canvas. Use the Magic Wand to select the green background. Hit delete.

Step 2

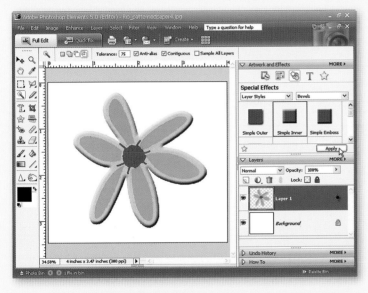

To add dimension, choose **Artwork and Effects palette>Layer Styles>Bevels>Simple Inner** (double-click on the starburst icon to customize the bevel layer) and click Apply.

Step 3

In the Artwork and Effects palette, choose **Layer Styles>Drop Shadows >Low** and click Apply. Delete the background layer.

Digital Frames

Almost any image looks better when framed. Fortunately, creating original frames digitally can be as simple as three steps.

The Rectangular Marquee and Elliptical Marquee tools are primarily used in making frames. To create your frame, you may select a portion of a background you have created, a piece of digital patterned paper, or even a photographic image. Whatever your choice, make sure you size your frames large enough to fit a variety of photos. To avoid distortion when resizing, it's a good idea to create square and rectangular versions of your frame.

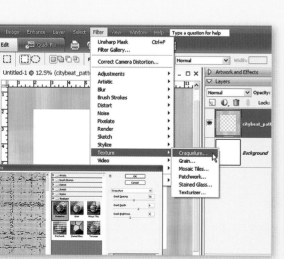

The Craquelure filter was applied to a digital frame created from a sheet of digital patterned paper to give the frame the look of crackled stone.

Photo: Jaime Coffman

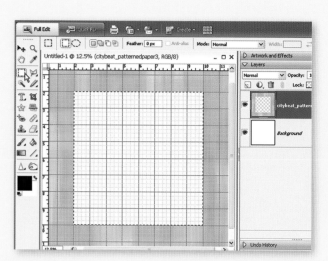

Step 1

Create a new colored layer or open a paper on a new layer (here we've used citybeat_patternedpaper3 from the CD). Choose the Rectangular Marquee tool to select the frame window and press Delete.

Step 2

To add the filter to the frame, choose **Select menu>Inverse**. Add texture (**Filter menu>Texture> Craquelure**) and adjust the sliders for your desired effect.

Step 3

To add dimension, choose **Artwork and Effects palette> Layer Effects>Bevels**, scroll down, choose Simple Inner and click Apply. Add a drop shadow (**Artwork and Effects palette>Layer Effects>Drop Shadows>Low**), if desired.

Digital Tags

Tags are as basic to scrapbook page design as photos. The beauty of tags is their versatility. Tags can hold a photo, contain a journaling block, give your page dimension, or simply add interest to a ho-hum design.

Like frames, tags are easy to create but often benefit from a personalized touch. In the step-by-step below, we show you not only how to create the tag but also how to give it some character. The inky edge added in the example is featured in the step-by-step below.

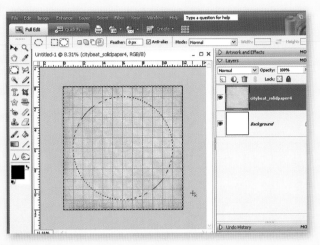

Step 1

Open a digital paper (here we've used citybeat_patterned paper4) on a new layer. Choose the Elliptical Marquee tool to create a circle (press Shift for a perfect circle). Choose **Select>Inverse** and hit Delete.

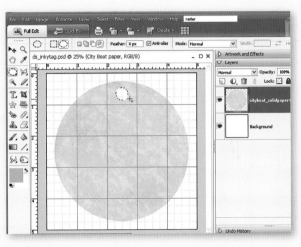

Step 2

Use the Elliptical Marquee tool to create a small tag hole at the top of the colored tag and press Delete.

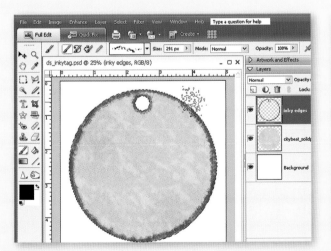

Step 3

To create the inky edges, create a new layer. Select the tag by pushing the Ctrl (mac: Cmd) key and clicking its thumbnail in the Layers palette. On the new layer, choose the Brush tool (here, the **Wet Media>Dry Brush on Towel** tip is used). Drag the brush around the edge of the tag and edge of the hole. Use the Eraser set to the same brush style to fine-tune the edges.

Step 4

For dimension, add a drop shadow (**Artwork and Effects palette>Layer Effects>Drop Shadows>Low**) to the tag layer. Delete the Background layer. The finished tag appears on p. 147.

Digital Metal and Plastic

Giving your accents or any digital surface the look of metal or plastic can be accomplished in a few simple steps. For the most realistic and customizable metal and plastic looks, apply Layer Effects. These affect the entire layer, so make sure the item you wish to alter is on its own layer.

Layer Effects are located in drop-down menu in the top left corner of the Artwork and Effects palette. Once Layer Effects are selected, the right drop-down menu will have Layer Effects categories, such as Pattern and Wow-Plastic. For the look of metal, try the Brushed Metal, Copper, and Diamond Plate styles in the Pattern category. For beveled chrome effects, look under the Wow-Chrome drop-down menu.

To add an effect, activate the layer, choose **Artwork and**

Effects palette>Layer Effects. Choose a category and scroll through the choices. Click on the one you want and then click Apply. You can customize your effect by choosing **Layer menu>Layer Effects>Style Settings**; a dialog box will open with adjustable sliders and options to add other basic effects. Cancel the effects by choosing **Layer menu>Clear Layer Effects**.

You can also use filters to create metallic effects. The Sketch filter (**Filter menu>Sketch**) offers a Chrome option that results in an artistic, although not quite realistic, metallic appearance.

For the illusion of plastic, the Wow-Plastic category of Layer Effects as well as some of the Glass Buttons effects will meet your needs. See the steps below and right to see these effects applied.

Digital scrapbookers can easily mimic the glossy, dimensional look of epoxy accents. This tag features a digital clear, epoxy bubble, which allows digital patterned paper to show from beneath it. See the instructions below to re-create the look.

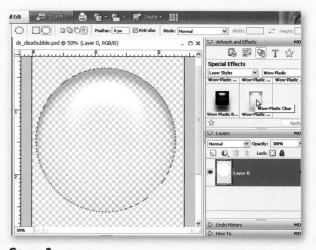

Leah Blanco Williams

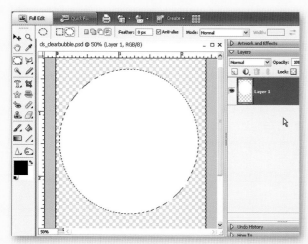

Step 1

On a new layer use the Elliptical Marquee tool to create a circle. Choose **Edit menu>Fill Selection** and choose white; click OK.

Step 2

In the Artwork and Effects palette, choose **Layer Effects>Wow-Plastic-Clear** and click Apply. Choose **Layer menu>Layer Effects>Style Settings**. In the dialog box, uncheck the Drop Shadow and Glow boxes to remove these effects; adjust the bevel as desired (for this 2.25" bubble, the bevel was set at 175 pixels).

Metal photo corners are a universal accent that can be used with layouts of all styles, from urban to shabby chic. The detail here shows how well the corner works with this distressed earth-tone paper. See p.149 for the entire image.

Heidi Knight

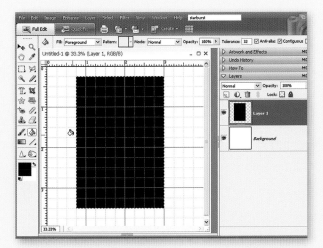

Step 1

On a new layer, create a rectangle shape with the Rectangular Marquee tool. Once drawn use the Paint Bucket tool to fill it with black or white.

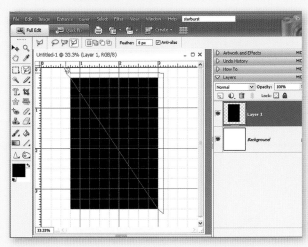

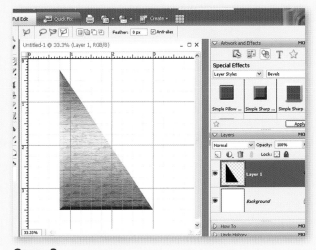

Step 2

Use the Polygonal Lasso tool to select half of the rectangle to create a triangle shape and hit Delete. From the Artwork and Effects palette, choose **Layer Effects>Patterns>Brushed Metal** and click Apply.

Step 3

Choose **Layer Effects>Bevels>Simple Sharp Inner** and apply. For a softer bevel, try Simple Inner. From the Artwork and Effects Palette, choose **Layer Effects>Shadows>Low** and apply. If desired, double-click the layer's starburst icon to customize the layer effects.

Toboggan Perfection

This toboggan hat is really mine, but I promise I do NOT mind you borrowing it. Besides, look how very adorable you look in it! I love how your eyes barely peek out from under it and how the black border highlights your pale skin and how the blue yarn makes your eyes just pop! Too cute! Oliver - Age 7

Shannon Taylor

The Digital Kit

Your digital supply stash begins with the CD included with this book. It includes four stunning and very unique digital kits created exclusively for you by our team of experienced digital kit designers. Their styles vary dramatically, which means you have the opportunity to explore a range of scrapbooking styles just by using these materials. In this chapter each artist demonstrates a variety of page layouts using her kit. The exercise will open your eyes to the bevy of design options at your fingertips.

You can further expand your collection of digital kits any time, day or night, seven days a week. The wonder of digital scrapbooking is that everything you need is available on the Internet, through the click of your mouse. You'll never find yourself bursting with inspiration and frustrated because you're unable to immediately turn your vision into a layout.

Detailing the strengths of digital scrapbooking kits could fill a book, but this chapter will introduce you to the highlights and give you the can-do confidence to move forward on your own.

Kit Basics
Making digital kits work for you

The styles of digital scrapbooking kits are endless, but most contain everything you need to create and embellish a scrapbook page. Because elements within a single kit are designed to work together, the guesswork of selecting compatible papers, photo corners, frames, accents, and journaling blocks is eliminated.

Quickpages

Along with traditional page elements, some digital scrapbooking kits include quickpages, or digital page templates (there are two included in each kit on the CD-ROM). These templates look like finished digital scrapbook pages. Elements have been sized, placed, and drop shadows have been applied. The only things missing are your photos and journaling. Size your images and then drag and drop them onto the template. Add a few words of your own, sit back, and admire your work. Digital scrapbooking doesn't get any easier than this!

Finding Digital Kits

Digital kits are available over the Internet (for a list of suggested Web sites, see p. 204). Most kits include four to eight pieces of digital patterned paper, a set of matching solid backgrounds, and a collection of accents. Many offer lettering sets as well as a brush set. Kits range in price, but most cost $4-$15. Many digital scrapbooking sites offer free downloadable kits. To find them, type "free digital scrapbooking kits" into your Internet search engine.

Most digital scrapbooking kits are composed of JPEG and PNG files, which are recognizable by almost all applications. The most popular image-editing programs used for digital scrapbooking (Adobe Photoshop/Photoshop Elements, Corel® Paint Shop Pro®, Corel DRAW®, Microsoft® Digital Image Suite, Ulead® PhotoImpact®) recognize these file formats. Typically, digital papers are JPEG files and accents are PNG files.

Page kits make scrapbooking a snap. This page was created with the Rio kit, which is included on the CD. All elements in the kit are digital, including patterned papers, ribbon, photo frames, swirls, summer accents (such as the sun), word art, and more. Everything matches, so you can be assured that your finished layouts will look beautiful.

Kimberly Giarrusso

Hunter loves to hang out in our backyard. He has the best time out there rolling in the grass, sunbathing, and watching the world go by. Today I had a chance to hang out with him and we had a great time together!

This page was created using a quickpage template (see below left) from the Street Fair kit on your CD. Open a new document and open the template. Open the photo as a new layer and use the Move tool to position the photo on top of the digital photo mat. To add journaling, create a new Type layer and format with leading and spacing to fit the prescribed journaling space on the template. Rearrange the layers as desired.

Erikia Ghumm

Erikia Ghumm

DIGITAL DIVAS KNOW

Protect yourself when you are searching for digital scrapbook goodies online. Free stuff often comes with strings attached. Don't give out credit card or bank information and never give your Social Security number to obtain free product. Also be careful about submitting your e-mail address as it can make you vulnerable to spam.

The Digital Marketplace

As you begin searching the Internet for products, you'll discover digital depots with the hot products and cool tutorials. You'll also become a part of a welcoming community of digital scrapbookers who are willing to answer questions and share layout inspiration. Message boards are popular among digital scrapbookers. Many artists post their layouts online for peer critiques. Constructive criticism and digital high-fives are doled out liberally. Many Web sites hold contests for scrapbookers. While the value of prizes vary, the opportunity to enter can offer incentive to keep developing your style and expertise.

Most Web sites, such as www.thedigichick.com and www.twopeasinabucket.com, have FAQ links that explain how to use the site, as well as site etiquette. For example, it's often considered rude to post more than five layouts a day since new layouts receive top billing. This ensures that all artists have an opportunity to participate. Compliments or criticism about displayed artwork should be carefully and sensitively worded. Artists posting layouts that were inspired by another scrapbooker's work should give credit where it is due.

Downloading Digital Kits

If you wish to download a digital scrapbooking kit from a Web site, you will be directed to a download page. Click the links to begin the download process. Most kits are compressed and need to be expanded or unzipped/un-stuffed (see p. 114 for more information on compressed files). While the process is usually straightforward, an error message or a password request indicates a problem. Most download problems are the result of a slow or interrupted Internet connection. Dial-up and wireless users are most susceptible to problems, and unfortunately there is no good solution. Problems can also be caused by firewalls you have installed and anti-virus applications. You can try to disable your firewall or anti-virus application long enough to download your files. Delete the problem file first and empty the trash before you attempt to download a second time.

Organizing Your Digital Kits

The key to kit organization is diligence. Make an effort to organize your kits as soon as they are downloaded. If you tend to create pages using elements from a single kit rather than mixing multiple kits, organize your supplies in a "kit" folder. Storing kits intact will also make it easier for you to identify elements, should you wish to submit your layouts for publication (publishers often wish to credit materials). Create the folder on your hard drive and drag your kits into it for storage. If you wish, you may break up your kits and organize them by components. Pull components (patterned papers, solids, brushes, frames, corners, mats, journaling blocks/strips, ribbon, buttons, brads, etc.) into labeled subfolders and store them in a kit folder on your hard drive.

Digital scrapbooking communities are an excellent place to find layout advice and like-minded people. At www.thedigichick.com, new users are invited to introduce themselves to the community so that they can make friends fast. Click on the Community link and under the "All Chicks Need to Know" heading, you will find the "New Chicks on the Block" link as well as the forum guidelines and FAQs. You can also find challenges, new products, and publication calls for layout submissions.

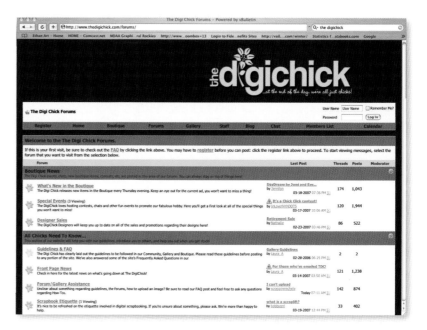

The artist of this page is an active member of the digital community. She hosts digital layout challenges called "Anything Goes" on www.thedigichick.com. Each week, a design team member posts a challenge and invites other Digichick members to participate. Layouts are posted and winners receive digital scrapbook elements.

Darla Velasquez

Uploading Layouts to the Web

If you decide to post your layouts to digital scrapbooking layout galleries, you must prepare the file by resizing and saving in a Web-friendly format.

- Flatten the file (**Layers palette>More>Flatten Image**) to eliminate layers and effects.

- Reduce the file size (**Image menu>Resize>Image Size**) by changing the resolution to 72 dpi and changing the dimensions to the Web site's specifications; click OK.

- If your page looks soft or fuzzy after resizing, choose **Enhance menu>Unsharp Mask** and drag the sliders until your page looks sharper; click OK.

- Choose **File menu>Save As** and choose the JPEG format. Choose a compression (High preserves the most data but has the largest file size), rename your file, choose a location, and click OK.

- For more control over JPEG settings (for example, preserving transparency), choose **File menu>Save for Web**. A dialog box will appear; choose JPEG (not GIF, which doesn't reproduce photographs well) and adjust the slider that controls compression. Compressing your file reduces it at the cost of image quality; 60 percent and higher (in regard to quality) is fine for Web publishing. Rename your file and click OK.

Our Digital Designers
Sharing their creativity

Four of the hottest designers in scrapbooking were chosen to create a collection of digital kits for you to use as you begin your scrapbooking journey (those kits can be found on the CD included with this book). The remaining pages of the book are dedicated to their insights. See how perseverance, luck, and creativity all played a part in their success. Peek into the creative world of each featured artist as she shares scrapbook pages from her heart and shows you the versatility of her kit with three unique ideas for each. For a full catalog of each kit element, see pp. 196 - 203.

Veronica Ponce

Veronica did not intend to become a professional scrapbooker. "I think the career found me as opposed to it being the other way around." Her success as an artist began when a national scrapbooking publisher requested a page she'd posted on a scrapbooking Web site for publication.

Following quickly were other publishing inquiries and offers to join a number of digital design teams. Her layouts have been featured in *Creating Keepsakes*, *Simple Scrapbooks*, and *Better Homes and Gardens* magazines as well as on www.scrapbookbytes.com and www.twopeasinabucket.com. When Autumn Leaves, a product manufacturer and publisher, asked her to be a freelance designer for their "Designing With" series, she was presented with her first opportunity to create a digital kit.

While Veronica's design work has generated its share of positive feedback, there is one compliment that she'll always cherish. "A person told me they could see my heart through my pages," she says. "The pages I create are a big part of me. Every single one of them goes into my family's memory books, so if others can see my heart, I hope that one day my kids will see it too."

Veronica lives with her husband, Carlos, and four kids in Miami, Florida.

On Veronica's scrapbook pages, the photos always trump any digital elements or techniques. The background for this page began as the photos. Veronica placed them on a diagonal and then "filled in" the design with strips cut from her patterned papers. After she added the journaling and title, she embellished the layout with her own digital flower elements.

Veronica Ponce

Veronica loves to blend photos with digital patterned paper to create backgrounds. This background consists of several merged layers. First, she adjusted the Hue/Saturation (**Enhance menu>Adjust Color>Adjust Hue/Saturation**) of the paper to match the photo. Then, she duplicated the photo layer twice, rotated the images slightly, and merged the two layers (hide layers you don't want to merge and choose **Layers palette>More>Merge Visible**). She then adjusted the opacity of the photo layer so the texture and color of the digital background paper would show through.

Veronica Ponce

Veronica's Favorite Digital Artists

Veronica says her "favorites" list could go on and on, but if push comes to shove, she absolutely loves…

Rhonna Farrar: Rhonna is a digital scrapbooking pioneer. She caused a stir in the industry at a time when some said digital scrapbooking would not catch on.

Anna Aspnes: I met her (online) years ago, and I have loved seeing her style and career evolve. She is constantly coming up with new and creative ideas, and I love that.

Tia Bennett: She is a creative genius. I think she has her finger on the pulse of digital scrapbooking, instinctively knowing what works and what doesn't. She is kind and outgoing and is just an extraordinary designer and woman.

Desiree McClellan: I have been admiring her work for years. I love her signature Desiree style. I don't think anyone comes close to what she can do with a page, in regard to graphics.

Erica Hernandez: She does an amazing job of making hybrid pages, which are scrapbook layouts that mix traditional and digital scrapbooking techniques, look easy. I constantly find myself looking at her pages and wondering, "How on earth did she come up with that?"

Anne Langpap: She makes the best "looks like paper" pages. Our styles are completely different, but I really like how she makes it work for her. She doesn't look like an imitation of anyone. Her papers are my favorite to work with.

One Kit Three Ways: City Beat

When Veronica designed her kit, City Beat, she knew its strength would lie in its texture and color palette. She loves how the gritty texture can add dimension and the fact that the color palette of the kit is universal. Veronica enjoys photo manipulation, collages, and the blending together of elements and colors; these techniques are apparent in the pages she's created with her kit. When beginning a layout, Veronica seldom has a concrete plan but always has a mood in mind. The emotion, not the design, dictates the direction in which her ideas travel. Although she loves the variety of pages she has created with her kit, she loves being surprised by the creativity others demonstrate when designing with her kits.

As a digital scrapbooker, Veronica loves to work with layers. It is through layer techniques that she develops her signature texture style. On this layout, she applied the texture from a digital paper to the focal photo. She loaded her digital papers as new fill patterns (see p. 154 for instructions). Then, she opened the photo and created a new Fill Layer (**Layer menu>Fill Layer**). After choosing the pattern, she experimented with the opacity until satisfied.

Veronica Ponce

If you are drawn to the texture or pattern of a digital paper, isn't it awesome that you can change the color of it to match any photo? Veronica adjusted the colors of some City Beat papers to better complement this photo. To alter the colors of any digital element, manipulate Hue/Saturation.

Veronica Ponce

Veronica Ponce

The design and concept of this layout mirrors Veronica's life as the happy mother of four. She mixed the bird and flower elements from the Street Fair kit with patterns and a swirl from the Rio kit with her own photos. She only altered the colors of the kit elements to match the mood of her page.

Displaying Your Finished Layouts

If you put your heart into your art, why not allow others to enjoy it, Veronica wonders? If you would like to display completed digital layouts, here are Veronica's ideas for three popular options to show off your digital scrapbook pages.

Slide shows: Most image-editing and image-organization applications have a Slide-show feature. Instructions vary from program to program, but most select layout files from the application's library and drop them into a new folder within the application (applications such as iPhoto will refer to the new folders as "albums"). Select the folder and choose the Slide-show feature. You can save and name your slide show; iPhoto, which is synched with iTunes, will allow you to put slide shows to music you have saved in your iTunes music library.

Online galleries: Post your layouts to digital scrapbooking Web sites to create a gallery of pages. Send family and friends the link so they can drop in for viewing.

Bound albums: If you don't own a large-format printer, but would like to showcase your layouts in a traditional album, you'll need to acquire the services of a professional. Type "digital scrapbook albums" into your Internet search engine to find companies that will print layouts and bind them into albums.

Kimberly Giarrusso

Kimberly has been scrapbooking in some form all her life, doodling on photos and journaling beside pictures in yearbooks. She took her first step into the digital realm when submitting a digital page in response to a challenge issued by a scrapbooking Web site. After that, she says, she was hooked. "When I started having children, I found it harder and harder to paper scrap," she says. "The time it takes to create a page and the mess were too much at the time. With digital scrapbooking, I am able to start a page and, if I need to walk away, I can save it and come back later."

Several months after going digital, Kimberly was invited to become a creative team member for a digital scrapbooking Web site. She began designing digital elements to support the site, and eventually introduced her own kit in 2005. Her designs are currently sold at her own store, www.purescrapability.com and sold at www.thedigichick.com. She considers it a compliment when people use her digital designs on their pages. "They could have bought any paper in the industry for their memory, and they chose mine," she says. "It's humbling."

Kimberly lives with her husband, Richard, whom she describes as "the person who inspires me most," and her four children, in Blythe, California.

When Kimberly creates pages, she wants to capture energy. This page is about her daughter, who is a total water baby. Kimberly identified a few themes in relation to the page: excitement, summer, and water fun. The patterns and repeating photo and button elements support the energetic photos of the toddling mermaid. To recreate a similar page, crop photos, pick four pieces of coordinating digital paper, and digitally trim with a Selection tool of your choice (for more information, see pp. 74 - 77). Arrange the papers and photos as desired and embellish with digital buttons and digital ribbon. The "K" tag was created from one of the Rio kit journaling blocks and a typed letter.

Kimberly Giarrusso

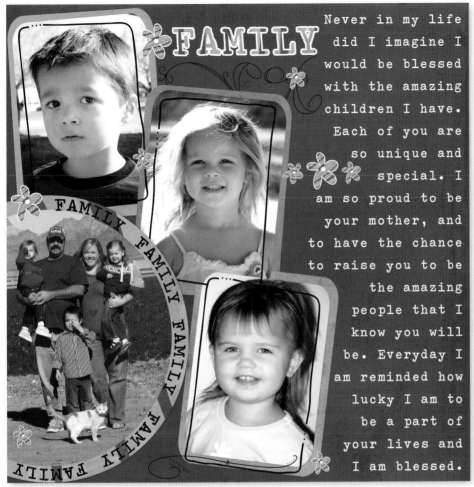

FAMILY

Never in my life did I imagine I would be blessed with the amazing children I have. Each of you are so unique and special. I am so proud to be your mother, and to have the chance to raise you to be the amazing people that I know you will be. Everyday I am reminded how lucky I am to be a part of your lives and I am blessed.

FAMILY FAMILY FAMILY FAMILY FAMILY FAMILY

Kimberly Giarrusso

Kimberly's scrapbook pages will be a source of family history, she says. Her wish is that her family, for generations to come, will use her scrapbook pages to remember the love shared between them. Digital kits make whipping up such layouts a pure snap. For this page created with the Rio kit, photos were cropped and matted onto digital paper that was trimmed to size. The title was cut from patterned paper as were the flower shapes. Digital doodles complete the design.

Q & A With Kimberly

Kimberly offers her two cents on a few topics.

Q: What image-editing program do you use? Why?
A: *I create with Photoshop. When I began digitally scrapbooking I tried many different programs, and I found that I am most comfortable using Adobe products. I tend to use keys to control what I am doing, and it's nice to have the consistency throughout the family of programs.*

Q: What is your favorite digital lifesaver?
A: *I have two digital lifesavers. First, I love using two computer monitors because they allow me to keep my Messenger window and all my Photoshop palettes on one screen while I design on the other. I also cannot live without my Wacom graphics tablet. Having the ability to hold the pen in my hand and draw gives me the freedom to create fun doodles that I could not have created with a mouse.*

Q: What is your creative process?
A: *I work backwards. I usually come up with the name of a kit before I create it, often at the same time that I am creating the color palette.*

Q: What is the best piece of advice you can give to new digital scrapbookers?
A: *Don't give up! There are so many tutorials and Web sites out there that cater to beginners. There are also Web sites that offer free trial image-editing programs. You don't need to spend a lot of money to get started in digital scrapping; you just need to have fun. It's a wonderful hobby, and the memories will last forever.*

One Kit Three Ways: Rio

Whether you are a busy mom with four kids, like Kimberly, or an artistic type with a full plate of life, digital scrapbooking makes it easy to be creative. There is so much freedom in being able to mix patterns, combine various elements from different kits, and alter digital elements to your liking. These are the very reasons that Kimberly loves the digital realm and the very benefits that her digital layouts illustrate. Plus, with digital scrapbooking, there is no cleanup; you can walk away from a project for months on end and no one's going to complain about the mess you left behind.

Elements from various kits are easy to mix when you find a common theme, Kimberly says. On this layout, a soft, distressed look ties together the elements from all four designers' kits, resulting in a feminine layout full of vim and vigor. All elements were used as is except for two. The color of the flower accent, from the Flutter kit, was altered via Hue/Saturation, and the photo frame, also from the Flutter kit, was transformed into a digital overlay (add the frame as a new layer, activate the layer, and choose Overlay from the drop-down menu in the Layers palette).

Kimberly Giarrusso

Have you flipped back to pp. 198 - 199 to see the Rio kit? Because the kit is so vibrant, it's hard to believe that this page was created with it, but it was. The colors for each of the digital elements used were altered by adjusting the Hue/Saturation.

Kimberly Giarrusso

A hot Blythe summer. The sun high in the sky, not a cloud in sight. A perfect day to go to the river. Today we went with cousins Joann and Bill. You had the best time on their boat. There isn't a better day spent than at the river. Packing a picnic, a bunch of drinks and a ton of sunscreen, these are the summers we remember. These are the summers you are going to cherish for the rest of your life. You have it good kid, and we love to watch you play, and swim and enjoy life. After all, this is what it's all about.

Kimberly Giarrusso

On this page, Kimberly digitally trimmed squares and strips from digital patterned paper with the Rectangular Marquee tool (for more information, see pp. 158 - 159), which she then layered on the background. The photo and journaling are the crowning touch.

Message Board Lingo

Internet communities love their abbreviated words. Digital scrapbookers are no different; Kimberly can attest to that fact. Here are some common abbreviations you may come across while surfing galleries and message boards:

BRB: be right back
DH: dear husband (DD: dear daughter; DS: dear son, etc.)
HTH: hope that helps
IRL: in real life
KWIM: know what I mean?

LOL: laugh out loud
MIL: mother-in-law (FIL: father-in-law; BIL: brother-in-law; SIL: sister-in-law)
PM: private message
RAK: random act of kindness
ROFL: rolling on the floor laughing
SB: scrapbooking
TTC: trying to conceive (a baby)
TFL: thanks for looking
TFS: thanks for sharing
TTYL: talk to you later

Erikia Ghumm

Erikia, a self-educated artist, was scrapbooking professionally before most people had even heard of the hobby. She began as a freelancer and then staff artist for *Memory Makers* magazine in 1999. While at *Memory Makers* she helped define hundreds of new trends in scrapbooking. She has contributed to more than 20 books and, after returning to freelancing, co-authored *Montage Memories* and authored *Tags Reinvented*. She is currently a contributing editor to Better Homes and Gardens' *Scrapbooking Etc.* magazine.

Erikia yearned to become an artist from the time that she was very small. The realization of her dream fills her with both pride and awe. She looks forward to continuing her work in both digital and traditional scrapbooking as well as other artforms. "I have set goals for myself and, once I reach them, I set more. I just keep reaching higher and higher," she says. "Although I feel as if I have sort of reached the top of my ladder, I still have things I want accomplish. I guess that it's time for me to grow wings and fly higher than my ladder can take me."

Erikia lives in Brighton, Colorado, with her husband, Brian, a cat, and a dog.

When it comes to creating art, Erikia alters most everything she touches, even the digital elements she designed for her kit. For the background, she layered a strip of solid purple paper over the pink doodle-patterned paper. She adjusted the opacity of the purple paper to soften it and to allow the pattern beneath to show. The photo edges were erased for a distressed look and doodles were added via a digital brush included in the kit. For more contrast, the bird and photo corner were converted to black and white.

Erikia Ghumm

Erikia loves to mix patterns and textures. For this background, the solid orange paper was layered over the mosaic-patterned paper and partly erased to reveal the mosaic pattern underneath. By decreasing the opacity of the mosaic pattern, it appears softer. An additional pattern was introduced on its own layer via digital brushes in different colors. Again, the opacity of this layer was decreased. On top of it all sits the photo, which receives definition from a distressed edge, which was created with a Photoshop Elements Default brush. Repeated star elements in various sizes complete the layout.

Erikia Ghumm

Take Erikia's Advice

Erikia is a seasoned designer, and here are some of her words of wisdom.

Build a solid foundation of knowledge: Don't rush through learning new techniques. Instead, spend as much time as necessary to hone skills before moving on to something new. It can be very frustrating to try to learn everything at once.

Work with layers: Whether working on images or digital layouts, layers will allow you to change and/or delete any part of the document without affecting the rest. Nothing is worse than having to start fresh because you didn't like one aspect of a design.

Save as you go: Computer freezes happen. Silly mistakes are made. If you save as you go, you will be assured work won't be lost.

Back up your files: If your hard drive crashes, your heart will break over your lost images and layouts. Invest in a backup plan for your work.

Save at least two copies of your work: Save a layered file so that you can re-edit at any time, and a flattened file for finished work.

Invest in equipment: Photoshop Elements is a fantastic program, but as you progress as a designer, move up to the latest version of Photoshop for the ultimate in creative control. I absolutely love my Epson printers. I have a C86 for printing text and printing on specialty media—I'll try printing on almost anything. I use a Stylus Photo 2200 for printing all of my photos and digital artwork. It has been worth investing in my Epson printers; I couldn't scrap without them.

One Kit Three Ways: Street Fair

Erikia is drawn to artists who have what she calls "a fearless approach to art." In her own designs, her style is evident, but rarely do any two pieces look alike. She loves strong and fantastic color stories as well as intriguing design concepts. When she creates pages, hardly anything is left in its native state. She is constantly distressing and altering. The layouts that follow demonstrate subtle tips and tricks that you can use to infuse your own art with individuality.

Imagine what a page would look like if a single accent captured the design focus. On this page, the star element in the Street Fair kit was reproduced in varying sizes. A super-sized star was created to layer on the background paper, resulting in eye-catching contrast.

Erikia Ghumm

Hybrid scrapbookers take the best from both the digital and traditional scrapbooking worlds to create stunning pages. For this layout, digital patterned paper and a digital page element (the bow) was printed onto white watercolor paper. The patterned papers were torn, distressed, and stamped upon to create the background. Then, the photos, the printed bow, a handwritten title, painted chipboard, and buttons were added to the layout. Dots of glitter glue add pizzazz to the stamped stitches on the green paper.

Erikia Ghumm

This Girl Loves...

OK, so I love to go shopping and I usually don't have a ton of money to spend, but really, that makes it fun! I scour the sales racks for bargains or I hit the thrift stores for cheap buys. You can find some of the most interesting things while doing this! And speaking of interesting things, I always get inspired while shopping. Today, not only did I score some new clothes, but I also got that cool bag shown above with a purchase!

to GO Shopping!

With all of its color and texture, using the Street Fair kit as the base for a multi-kit mix seems challenging. But here the result is a wonderful collection of layers. The background begins with a Street Fair pattern. Then the flower element from the City Beat kit was introduced as its own layer (the Hue/Saturation was adjusted to turn the flower green and then the opacity was reduced to help it blend into the background). To help the photos pop off the background, they were matted on the Street Fair solid purple paper, which was made more saturated via Hue/Saturation. The swirl element from the Flutter kit was added near the edges of the photo (one of the swirls was flipped, see p. 83 for instructions). Finally, the Street Fair flower and corner elements were added, and on top of the flower rests a button from the Rio kit (the Hue/Saturation was adjusted to turn it magenta).

Erikia Ghumm

Digital Scrapbooking and Beyond

Erikia can often be found creating treasured memory crafts with her digital skills. This is just a sampling of her ideas:

Family cookbook: Your family history can be traced through original recipes, dinnertime and holiday traditions, and favorite comfort foods. Use image-editing software to create a family cookbook. Build a layout template that can be repeated throughout the book. The layouts should include a recipe's list of ingredients and instructions and, if desired, space for family photos and memories. Enrich the cookbook with family anecdotes that tell any special details about the recipes, mealtime traditions, and fond family stories. Have the pages laminated to protect them from spills and splashes.

Calendar: No home is complete without a calendar to keep track of family life. But why spend money to spend the year looking at someone else's photographs when you can look at your own for free? Microsoft Word calendar templates can be found online and downloaded for free. Print the templates and then design a decorative counterpart for each month. Use adorable family photos, your own experimental photography, or your favorite scrapbook layouts to decorate your calendar.

Photo art: Your hard drive is no doubt brimming with digital images just waiting to be altered, and not all images need to be destined for a scrapbook page. Print family photos onto canvas. Use the Impressionist Brush tool to transform a beautiful vista into a masterpiece. Collage printed heirloom photos onto an old cigar box that you can then fill with family memorabilia, such as service badges and antique jewelry. Use photos of your family, dolls' clothing, and found objects to create representative figures that can be displayed in a family shrine.

Jackie Eckles

Jackie first began as a traditional scrapbooker, but after casually picking up a copy of a digital scrapbooking magazine, she became hooked on the digital realm. She says she was seduced by the speed with which she could create layouts and the ability to "fix" artwork after reconsidering creative choices.

She began designing her own digital products in 2006. "I loved working with other designers' product, but was always missing some element or paper that I could not find to buy, so I began making them," she says. "Most of my first attempts have been sacrificed by the mighty Delete button, but once I had some things I liked, I showed them to some friends and was given the opportunity to start designing." Jackie currently creates digital designs for Designer Digitals and Autumn Leaves.

Jackie says her creative process relies on listening to her "inner artist" and drawing inspiration from things that compel her, including her photos, the artwork of others, and beautiful vistas. She advises scrapbookers to follow their own muses and to discover their own personal styles.

Jackie, her husband, Edward, and two sons, live in College Place, Washington.

When Jackie creates a page, she feels as every scrapbooker should: Everything touched by her is her because it comes from her. Jackie loves working with layers. To create this background, she layered two background papers on top of each other (Flutter papers 1 & 4), adjusting the Hue/Saturation to increase the vibrancy of the red and adjusting the opacity to allow the lower pattern to show through. She created a wall of photos, each with a distinct color variation. Underneath the photos, she placed several flowers, a digital swirl, and photo frame so that they would peek out from beneath.

Jackie Eckles, Photo: Edward Eckles

Jackie is the mother of two lovely sons, and she wants them to remember the little details of life. When she creates a page, journaling is important because it tells the story. Text was easily added to these digital journaling strips. Position strips as desired onto the page background. Choose the Type tool and customize the settings as desired in the Options bar. Position the tool over the journaling strips and type. A new text layer will be created.

Jackie Eckles

Jackie's Inner Digital Designer

Is it magic, or do the most creative designers have a secret? Find out what helps make Jackie an elite designer.

"When I design a page, I strive to create a natural flow that encourages the reader's eye to move around the page. Visual triangles are great tools to accomplish this. Position key page elements, such as the title, focal photo, and journaling, on the layout so that they exist as the points of the triangle. Or, use a 'Z' formation. Arrange key elements so that the reader's eye begins at the top left of the layout and follows elements across the layout in a 'Z' pattern.

"Often, I step outside of my comfort zone. It causes me to become a stronger designer. Generally, I prefer clean and linear layouts but, for this book, I was asked to create a digital kit with some distressing. At first it seemed a little counterintuitive, but I surprised myself with the results and feel I have grown as an artist because of it.

"If, when finished with a layout, something doesn't seem right, I will try subtracting elements from it instead of adding to it. Many times a layout will benefit from simplifying the design. For example, I might try covering up page elements and photos with other layers and then slowly uncovering them until I find a look I like.

"The Brush tool is my all-time favorite digital tool because it is a great way to add extra dimension to a digital layout! Get to know your Brush tool. I love to experiment with a given brush's Opacity and Scatter settings. Once I've applied the brush pattern or texture to my layout, I will erase bits of it or make selections from it to use elsewhere. I store them in folders based on the Web site from which I either bought or downloaded them. That way, if I really like the style, I know where to return to look for new ones.

"Fonts are another area in which I love to experiment. Usually, I will highlight my text and then scroll through my fonts on the Options bar until I find just the right one. Then, I'll start adding color, maybe a little texture. Time flies when I'm having some font fun!

"Get involved in the digital community. It's such a welcoming environment, and it will, without a doubt, help you improve your design skills. There is always a challenge to inspire and push you to your creative limits."

One Kit Three Ways: Flutter

This kit shows the melding of two worlds: our everyday reality and the fanciful musings of our mind. The design foundation is equal parts precision and scribbles. This is somewhat of a departure for Jackie, who tends to design in a linear fashion. But with every challenge comes growth, she says. These three pages show a moment of growth for Jackie as, like her kit, they are a perfect blending of two styles: a little bit grungy, a little bit clean and graphic. While the collection shows unity in regard to page style, look for the subtle nuances in technique, for learning them will make your own pages shine with brilliance.

Hands down, Jackie's favorite digital tool is the brush. She also loves the Eraser tool, which has a brushlike tip that can be customized as desired. As you can see in this layout, you can add texture to a layout using the Eraser tool to distress elements. Jackie paired the Eraser tool with the Natural Brushes 2 tip (select from the Brush Style drop-down menu in the Options bar) and then dragged the brush across the title and page background.

the search for easter eggs and a quick check to see how many

Liam - Age four

eggs

Jackie Eckles

of those photos one of those moments

moments

a beautiful day - a beautiful moment with my little one

Jackie Eckles, Photo: Edward Eckles

Any digital element you download, purchase, or find on the CD that was included in this book can be made into a digital brush (for more information, see pp. 104 - 107). With the brush, you can repeatedly stamp the design and customize its shape, angle, size, and texture. On this layout, Jackie created brushes from the swirls and the butterfly overlay in her kit. She then used the brushes to stamp the designs on successive new layers. To create depth, she adjusted the opacity of the various layers.

On this layout, linear design meets distressed textures. Jackie used a grunge strip from the City Beat kit along the right side of her page. From the Rio kit, she used the black frame, button, and sun. To convert the sun from warm orange to cool blue, she adjusted the Hue/Saturation. She then adjusted the opacity to make it transparent. She layered a strip of her own patterned paper on top and also adjusted the opacity so the sun could peek through.

THREE HAPPY FACES

My happy little felllas - while trying to get a 'mug-shot' photo for Cantata, the boys jumped in, too - smiles and laughs always a fun bunch - they goof - making sure you say cheese - tickle you to make sure you smile...

Jackie Eckles, Photos: Edward Eckles

So You Want to Be a Digital Designer...

Guess what? The goal is more attainable than you think. Here are some tips from all four kit artists:

Listen to your inner artist: All four kit designers for this book agreed that this was the best piece of constructive criticism they have ever received regarding their work.

Self-taught designers are the norm, not the exception: Most digital designers, including the four featured in this book, do not have a background in graphic design. They have soldiered through learning digital techniques by using online tutorials, getting advice from friends, and reading computer manuals. Some have gone pro within only a year of becoming a digital scrapbooker.

Put your work out there: Digital design-team managers and magazine and book editors scour the online galleries looking for new talent. Find digital scrapbooking sites and create a gallery. Keep it updated. Sign up for digital scrapbooking newsletters; they often post calls for entries, contests, and challenges. Submit.

Network with other designers: Seek advice from designers you admire. Most will be flattered you find their work meaningful.

Critique the work of others: Pay attention to other designers and offer constructive criticism when they request it. As you evaluate the work of others, you'll learn to better evaluate your own. Allow others to critique your work as well.

Challenge yourself: Continue experimenting and developing new techniques.

Awesome Designer Digital Kits
Unlocking their possibilities

Seeing is believing, so, we've set aside the next eight pages to show you how beautiful these digital kits are. As phenomenal as they are, simply allow them to be a starting point for your own digital creativity instead of relying on them for your layout punch. You'll find the kits on the CD, organized in their own separate folders by kit name.

City Beat

City Beat is soft, but not too soft. Trendy. Worn. Textured. Dimensional. That's how this kit's designer, Veronica Ponce, describes her work. The kit features subtle motifs and a gender-neutral palette. It draws scrapbookers who love clean, graphic, or urban styles, and works well with themes about everyday life or contemplative topics.

Patterned Papers

citybeat_patternedpaper1

citybeat_patternedpaper2

citybeat_patternedpaper3

citybeat_patternedpaper4

citybeat_patternedpaper5

citybeat_patternedpaper6

Solid Papers

citybeat_solidpaper1

citybeat_solidpaper2

citybeat_solidpaper3

citybeat_solidpaper4

Quickpages and Accents

citybeat_quickpage1

citybeat_motifstamp

citybeat_flower

citybeat_grid

citybeat_wordart1

citybeat_wordart2

citybeat_wordart3

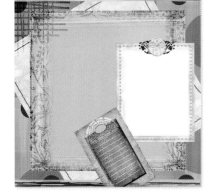

citybeat_quickpage2

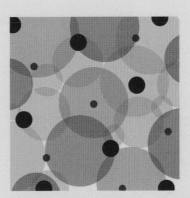

citybeat_journalingtag

citybeat_frame

citybeat_corners

citybeat_grungestrip

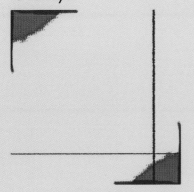

citybeat_ribbons

citybeat_brad1   citybeat_brad2

citybeat_datestamp

citybeat_meshribbon

Overlays

citybeat_overlay1

citybeat_overlay2

citybeat_overlay3

Rio

Rio's papers and elements were created in the dead of winter while the artist longed for summer. The resulting kit left Kimberly Giarrusso filled with warmth and a sense of fun.

As she developed the color palette and textures, she drew inspiration from fabric, the desert sky, and the décor inside a Japanese-fusion restaurant. This is just the kit for pages that call for vibrant, playful, summery, and sassy backdrops.

Patterned Papers

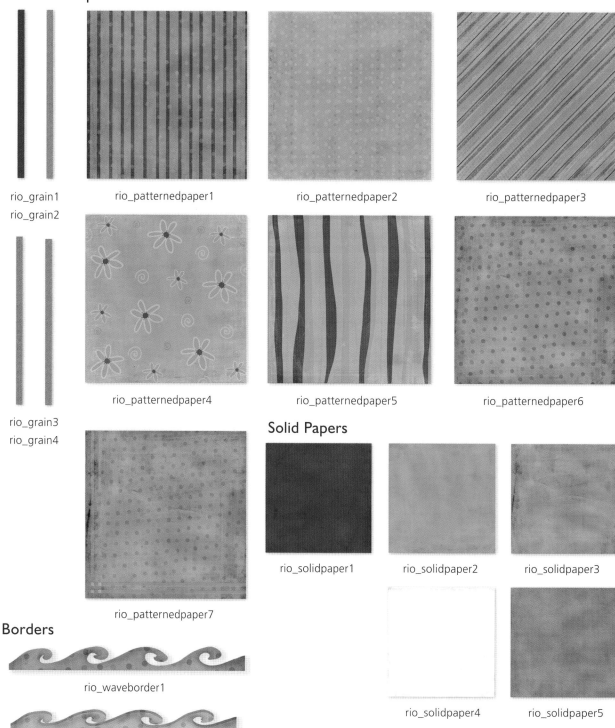

rio_grain1
rio_grain2

rio_patternedpaper1

rio_patternedpaper2

rio_patternedpaper3

rio_patternedpaper4

rio_patternedpaper5

rio_patternedpaper6

rio_grain3
rio_grain4

Solid Papers

rio_patternedpaper7

rio_solidpaper1

rio_solidpaper2

rio_solidpaper3

rio_solidpaper4

rio_solidpaper5

Borders

rio_waveborder1

rio_waveborder2

Quickpages and Accents

rio_quickpage1

rio_quickpage2

rio_journaltagorange

rio_journaltagblue

rio_chipbracket

rio_blueblock

rio_buttonblue
rio_buttongreen
rio_buttonorange
rio_buttonred
rio_groovyflower

rio_orangecircle
rio_triangle
rio_diamond
rio_glitterflower

rio_sunshine
rio_beach
rio_oval
rio_waves

rio_umbrella
rio_spiral
rio_xstaple
rio_staple
rio_filetab

rio_sun
rio_sunglasses
rio_beachball
rio_pail

rio_greenblock

rio_frameblue

rio_shovel

Overlays (also available as brushes)

rio_4x6frame_blk

rio_doodlerectangle

rio_doodleflower3
rio_doodleflower4

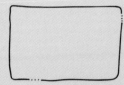

rio_doodlecircle
rio_swoosh
rio_flourish

rio_doodleflower1
rio_doodleflower2
rio_doodleswirl

rio_4x6frame_wht

rio_doodlesquare

Street Fair

Street Fair's designs were inspired by two seemingly incompatible scenes: the artist's urban back alley and her garden. Erikia Ghumm put her favorite mediums—acrylic paint, inks, and other diverse colorants—to paper before transforming them into digital designs. Erikia, a true multimedia maven, also included doodles, hand-cut elements, and handmade stamps to create the stylish motifs. This digital kit is an excellent choice for celebratory layouts.

Patterned Papers

streetfair_patternedpaper1

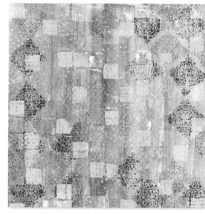
streetfair_patternedpaper2

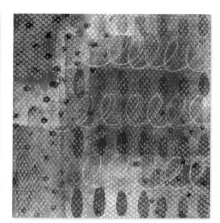
streetfair_patternedpaper3

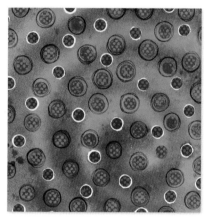
streetfair_patternedpaper4

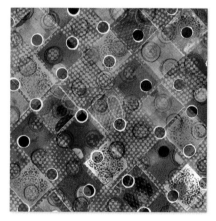
streetfair_patternedpaper5

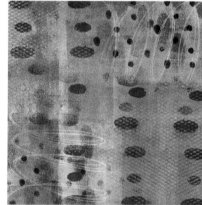
streetfair_patternedpaper6

Solid Papers

streetfair_solidpaper1

streetfair_solidpaper2

streetfair_solidpaper3

streetfair_solidpaper4

Quickpages

streetfair_quickpage1

streetfair_quickpage2

Accents

streetfair_textcorner1 - 4

streetfair_doodlecorner1 - 4

streetfair_tag

streetfair_bird

streetfair_bow

streetfair_star

streetfair_butterfly

streetfair_flower

Brushes (streetfair.abr)

Flutter

Butterflies and doodles are the things from which daydreams are made. This kit by Jackie Eckles has a soft color palette and is a departure from her usual vibrant style, but she loved the challenge of creating something utterly different and new. Motifs, tempered with the ruled lines of notebook paper, take you back to school-day afternoons spent staring longingly out the window. The hand-rendered designs give the collection an innocence that translates well for carefree, feminine, romantic, and nature-inspired layouts.

Patterned Papers

flutter_patternedpaper1

flutter_patternedpaper2

flutter_patternedpaper3

flutter_patternedpaper4

flutter_patternedpaper5

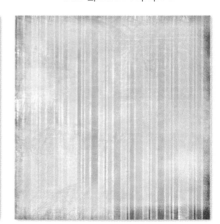
flutter_patternedpaper6

Solid Papers

flutter_solidpaper1

flutter_solidpaper2

flutter_solidpaper3

flutter_solidpaper4

Quickpages and Accents

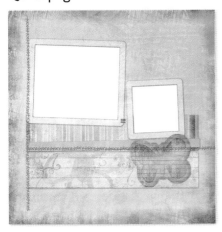

flutter_quickpage1

flutter_quickpage2

flutter_flower1

flutter_flower2

flutter_pageborder

flutter_label1
flutter_label2
flutter_label3
flutter_label4

flutter_butterfly1   flutter_butterfly3
flutter_butterfly2   flutter_butterfly4

flutter_frame1

flutter_frame2

flutter_journalstrip

Overlays

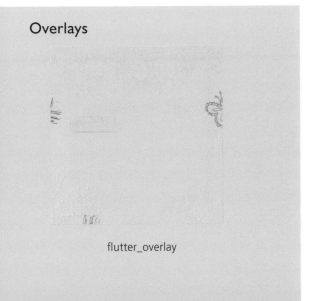

flutter_overlay

flutter_swirl1

flutter_swirl2

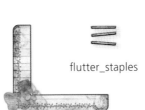

flutter_photocorner1

flutter_staples

flutter_photocorner2

flutter_button

Resources

Digital Scrapbooking

The following Web sites are great places to connect with other digital scrapbookers, shop, and find digital scrapbooking technique tutorials:

Club Scrap Digital
www.clubscrap.com

Computer Scrapbook
www.computerscrapbook.com

Daisie Company
www.daisiecompany.com

Designer Digitals
www.designerdigitals.com

The Digi Chick
www.thedigichick.com

Digi Scrap Divas
www.digiscrapdivas.com

Digi Shop Talk
www.digishoptalk.com

Digital Freebies
www.digitalfreebies.com

Digital Scrapbook Pages
www.digitalscrapbookpages.com

Digital Scrapbook Place
www.digitalscrapbookplace.com

Random Acts of Kindness Scraps
www.rakscraps.com

Scrapbook Bytes
www.scrapbook-bytes.com

Scrapbook Elements
www.scrapbook-elements.com

Scrapbook Flair
www.scrapbookflair.com

Scrap Girls
www.scrapgirls.com

Scrapjazz
www.scrapjazz.com

The Shabby Shoppe
www.theshabbyshoppe.com

Sweet Shoppe Designs
www.sweetshoppedesigns.com

Two Peas in a Bucket
www.twopeasinabucket.com

Digital Scrapbooking Tools

Check out these Web sites for software and other helpful digital products:

Adobe: Photoshop, Photoshop Elements, InDesign, fonts, web, desktop publishing, and image-editing software
www.adobe.com

Apple Computer: MacIntosh computers and photo software
www.apple.com

Corel: Graphics, Web, desktop publishing, and image-editing software
www.corel.com

Epson: Printers, papers, scanners, and digital scrapbooking tips
www.epson.com

Hallmark: Scrapbook Studio digital scrapbooking software
www.hallmarksoftware.com

Hewlett-Packard: Printers, papers, scanners, and digital scrapbooking tips
www.hp.com

Lexmark: Printers, papers, and scrapbooking tips
www.lexmarkstore.com

Lumapix: FotoFusion digital scrapbooking software
www.lumapix.com

Memory Mixer: Digital Scrapbooking/Multimedia Software
www.memorymixer.com

Microsoft: Business software and digital scrapbooking tips
www.microsoft.com

Nova Development: Art Explosion Scrapbook Factory Deluxe digital scrapbooking software
www.novadevelopment.com

PhotoMix: Digital scrapbooking and collage software
www.photomix.com

Scrapbook Max: Digital scrapbook album software
www.scrapbookmax.com

Shutterfly: Online digital album-printing services
www.shutterfly.com

Ulead: PhotoImpact image-editing software
www.ulead.com

Wacom: Graphics tablets
www.wacom.com

Fonts
Great sites for free and high-quality type faces

1001 Free Fonts
www.1001freefonts.com

1001 Fonts
www.1001fonts.com

Acidfonts
www.acidfonts.com

Adobe
www.adobe.com

Dafont.com
www.dafont.com

Dingbat Depot
www.dingbatdepot.com

Font Freak
www.fontfreak.com

Free Fonts
www.free-fonts.com

MyFonts
www.myfonts.com

P22
www.p22.com

SearchFree Fonts.com
www.searchfreefonts.com

Simply the Best Fonts
www.simplythebest.net/fonts

Veer
www.veer.com

Other Resources
A variety of online resources for all scrapbookers

Cantata Books: Scrapbooking and craft books, getting your scrapbook page published, scrapbooking supplies
www.cantatabooks.com

Genealogy.com: Genealogy tips, free searches, family-tree and family history software
www.genealogy.com

The Quote Garden: Quotes, sayings, verses, and poems arranged by topic
www.quotegarden.com

Scrapbook Addict: Scrapbooking community, tips, links, buy/sell scrapbooking supplies
www.scrapbookaddict.com

Scrapbooking Obsession: Apparel and home goods for the enthusiastic scrapbooker
www.scrapbookingobsession.com

ScrapLink: Links to all types of scrapbooking-related sites, including clipart, fonts, clubs, photo services, and products
www.scraplink.com

The Taunton Press: Publishers of craft and how-to books and magazines on a variety of subjects
www.taunton.com

Jackie Eckles, Photo: Rebecca Russell

Index

Index